BEHIND THE SCENES OF
NASCAR
RACING

WILLIAM BURT

$\mathrm{M \! B \! I}$

This edition first published in 2003 by
Motorbooks International, an imprint of MBI
Publishing Company, Galtier Plaza, Suite 200,
380 Jackson Street, St. Paul, MN
55101-3885 USA

The information in this book is true and
complete to the best of our knowledge. All
recommendations are made without any
guarantee on the part of the author or
publisher, who also disclaim any liability
incurred in connection with the use of this
data or specific details.

We recognize that some words, model names,
and designations, for example, mentioned
herein are the property of the trademark
holder. We use them for identification
purposes only. This is not an official
publication.

Motorbooks International titles are also
available at discounts in bulk quantity for
industrial or sales-promotional use. For details
write to Special Sales Manager at Motorbooks
International Wholesalers & Distributors,
Galtier Plaza, Suite 200, 380 Jackson Street,
St. Paul, MN 55101-3885 USA.

ISBN 0-7603-1458-6

On the front cover: *Left:* Terry Labonte's crew
pushes his car through the garage area.
Center: Jimmie Johnson performs one of a
NASCAR driver's primary duties: serving as
the voice and face for his race team.
Right: Kevin Harvick's crew makes last
minute preparations to his car before a race.
Cover photos courtesy Nigel Kinrade

On the frontispiece: When qualifying is
complete, the cars are directed back off of
the track.

On the title page: The starting field of the
2002 Daytona 500 prepares to take to the
track. *Nigel Kinrade*

On the back cover: *Left:* Bobby Labonte's
crew rolls out the #18 Joe Gibbs Pontiac.
Lower right: Once the cylinder heads for this
race motor are bolted on (with the valves and
valve springs already installed), the rest of the
valvetrain is assembled. *Upper right:* With so
many days spent on the road, drivers like Bill
Elliott have to find time to spend with their
families whenever they can.

Edited by Peter Bodensteiner
Designed by LeAnn Kuhlmann

Printed in China

CONTENTS

INTRODUCTION

When Bill France settled in Daytona more than half a century ago, there was no way that he could know what his dreams of organized stock-car racing would produce. During the early years of NASCAR was truly "stock-car" racing. The models on the track were closed based on those on the road.

NASCAR officially recognizes the 1972 season as the beginning of its "Modern Era." Two major changes took place. First, a new points system was introduced (a system that remains to this day). Second, RJR began its sponsorship of the entire series, renaming NASCAR's Grand National Championship the Winston Cup Championship.

The next era of Winston Cup racing began in the late 1980s and early 1990s. Stock-car racing for decades had been a sport of trial and error. Setups were primarily based on previous race experience and a bit of testing. But in this era, science and technology became more important to successful race teams. While items such as carbon fiber chassis, turbochargers, and electronic engine control became commonplace in other racing venues, NASCAR racers stayed much the same as they had always been. They kept their steel chassis, carburetors, and engine-driven distributors, but teams began to use more science and technology in the continuing refinement of these antiquated systems.

While racers have always tried (sometimes by cheating) to make their cars better and faster, by the early nineties NASCAR's rulebook and inspection procedures were much more thorough. It was not possible to come up with one revolutionary idea that would give a team a significant advantage. So began a campaign to make small improvements in all areas of the car's performance.

To be competitive, each of these systems had to be refined to a high degree. The sophisticated tools necessary to do this soon followed. Computer-controlled machining capabilities allowed teams to lighten and improve the performance of parts. Wind-tunnel testing helped teams refine the downforce and drag of the body. Coordinate measuring machines could measure everything from the smallest parts to the entire body with incredible accuracy. Dynamometers and Spintrons gave more feedback to engine builders without going to the track.

By this time, the demands of racing had made stock components inadequate. Every bit of the car was either custom-built or purchased from a high-quality aftermarket source. Parts today are inspected and reinspected by both the manufacturers and the teams. Before many parts ever touch the car, they are inspected by X-ray, penetrating dyes, and computerized measuring devices.

As the sport heads into the future, the rulebook will only get tighter and the teams will continue to look for their competitive advantage through small changes. The result is that talent throughout the team will be at a premium. The fastest cars will be built by the most talented, most open-minded teams.

2002 Winston Cup Champion Tony Stewart leads teammate Bobby Labonte around the twisting road course at Sears Point in California. *Nigel Kinrade*

CHAPTER ONE

THE BUSINESS OF RACING

An electric fuel pump died on me once near Silverthorne, Colorado, while I was traveling through the Rocky Mountains. Fortunately, I found a small shop that had the right one in stock. The shop's owner, a grizzled Vietnam veteran, had a few of those little two-seat Datsuns—the ones that look like MGs—prepped for Sports Car Club of America (SCCA) road racing. I was young, fresh out of school, and, but for a complete lack of money, would have been knee-deep in amateur racing. So, of course, we talked about racing.

I don't remember the shop owner's name, but when he learned I was interested in racing, he said something that I will never forget. "You need to choose between hard drugs and racing, but know that the result is about the same. You'll piss away all of your money for a little bit of a high, and there is a chance you might get killed." He looked away pensively and

By attracting large crowds, extensive television coverage, and sponsorship from major corporations, NASCAR racing has emerged as a profitable business opportunity for many team owners.

While NASCAR has grown out of its amateur roots, dirt tracks throughout the country offer racers a chance to revisit them. Every Saturday night, amateur team owners spend their hard-earned money fielding their racing efforts.

continued: "I probably preferred the hard drugs, because at least with them I never had to pull a trailer."

Now, I'm not suggesting that you head out and do drugs, but there is a certain logic to his theory. Racing is a very expensive form of entertainment at any level, amateur or professional. From the pony cars that run on dirt tracks all across America up to the likes of Formula One vehicles, Indy cars, and, of course, the National Association for Stock Car Auto Racing (NASCAR), a remarkable amount of money is spent. These days, most who enter the world of Winston Cup ownership are already wealthy.

Above and opposite top: Joe Gibbs brought to NASCAR the people skills that made him successful in the National Football League. By 2000, he had won a championship. The great quarterback Dan Marino's Winston Cup effort was not as successful and faded away within a couple of years.

Wealth, though, assures nothing. There is an old adage that says, "When it comes to racing, the quickest way to have a million dollars in the bank is to start with $10 million." Money can fly through a Winston Cup team fast enough to make even the wealthiest cringe. In fact, if you take a look at today's successful teams, you'll see that most of them have been around a while. Organizations like Woods Brothers Racing and Petty Enterprises have been racing almost since the beginning of NASCAR, and they continue to win. Other teams, like Joe Gibbs racing and Dale Earnhardt, Inc. (DEI), were formed more recently but have also found great success.

In the last decade, a number of wealthy folks who decided to race in NASCAR have been in and out within a year or two. It is not so much a difficult sport to enter as it is a difficult sport to *survive*. Starting a team is an expensive proposition, but with enough cash, anyone can do it. Success, however, takes much more than cash. It takes abilities such as leadership, vision, and people skills.

Building a Team

So what does it take to build a team, besides money? An owner must first assemble an organization to lead. He must buy or build a shop; have on hand all of the tools and equipment necessary to build, test, and maintain the race cars; and hire the all of the necessary personnel to prepare and race the cars and to run the team on a day-to-day basis. Buying an existing team is the quicker and probably least-expensive route. When the transaction is complete, the new owner has buildings, equipment, cars, and, perhaps, employees. Starting from scratch takes much longer, and this approach usually means that the owner buys everything new, which is why it is typically the more expensive method.

Creating a race team from the ground up usually ensures that you will get what you want, but the buck doesn't stop there. There are a minimum of thirty or forty guys to pay every week, a steady stream of materials to purchase, plus the actual racing costs. One simple pit stop costs almost $2,000 in materials alone. Drivers, good team members, parts,

In racing, any competitor can be put out of the event by circumstances well beyond his control. The first-place car's day can easily be ended by a car running 20 laps down. One never knows what to expect until the checkered flag is waved.

cars, transporters, machining centers, and publicity photos all cost money. The act of getting the team to the track every week costs money. Everything costs money.

So, like any business, revenue is the first critical element. Simply winning money at the track will not come close to covering the bill. There will be weekends when the primary car is wrecked in practice and the team qualifies

In the 1950s, cars were strictly stock, and many a man was disqualified for the slightest of modifications. *International Motorsports Hall of Fame*

poorly in the backup car or wrecks early and finishes dead last. Deep pockets may be essential, but lining them early and often strictly from winnings is an impossible task in today's NASCAR.

By the 1960s, the cars were still stock, but a few modifications were allowed.

Money

For years, the primary companies to sponsor race cars and racing were automotive product outfits and beer and tobacco makers. STP, Purolator, Budweiser, R. J. Reynolds, and Miller recognized long before others the potential advantages of associating themselves with the fast-paced action of NASCAR racing.

As the sport's popularity grew, larger crowds flocked to events and television became a powerful player for NASCAR. With this, the demographics of the NASCAR fan changed. No longer was the "typical" fan the beer-lov-ing Saturday mechanic. The new-found NASCAR nation included folks from all walks of life, and one result of this was the mass diversification of sponsors. While the old standbys were still visible on race day, scores of companies anxious to gain far-reaching expo-sure for their products hopped onto the hood of NASCAR racing. Today, brand names of everything from pantyhose to sexual-enhance-ment drugs to laundry detergent radiate prominently from any car and every venue.

These dramatic increases in crowds, televi-sion audiences, and sponsor interest—not to

The requirement to stay with the stock body led to manufacturers introducing "special" models that were available to the general public, like Dodge's "winged" Daytona.

mention merchandising—fueled a surge in interest and product demand paralleled in very few industries. With this interest and demand came money. Big money. Money that could be used on cars, on testing, on everything. More money to win each weekend raised the stakes even higher. It wasn't long before a team and driver *had* to have money, and lots of it. Consider that in the early 1970s, a budget of $50,000 was enough to run the circuit. In the 1980s, $500,000. In the 1990s, $1 to $5 million. Today, $10 million! Where do teams get that kind of money?

NASCAR, Inc.

What you see on the track is only part of the NASCAR story. The other part is the "business of NASCAR." Long before its car hits the track, a team's success is influenced by activities in corporate headquarters throughout the country. Team owners and managers meet with large corporations, and the result is the "200-mile-per-hour billboard." The revenue to support a Winston Cup team is paid by sponsors who are betting on the fact that a good, competitive effort from the team will mean more attention and more exposure. The better the team, the more airtime a sponsor's logo will receive during the weekend, both during the race and in interviews with the driver and team members. Sponsors often contract other companies to record how many times their car is on camera, how many times the company name is mentioned, and so on. Thus, the sponsor can compare this to advertising costs and come up with some idea of its return.

After landing a primary sponsor, the team will recruit associate sponsors to try and cover as much of the car as possible with advertisements. Stickers on different parts of the car demand different prices. The post behind the driver's window, which is visible when an interview is done with the driver sitting in the car, goes for about a $500,000. Deck lids and the lower rear fender areas are other top

In the 1970s, the cars began to make the transition from stock models altered for racing to racing cars built with stock parts.

associate sponsor spots, and placement here may cost a million dollars or so. From a sponsor's perspective, the space on a car is like a farmer's field: The more you can plant, the better the return.

Teams have a winning formula when they can combine the big dollars of their sponsors with good personnel. More money means more testing, more experimentation, better equipment in the shop, and, often, better results. Big dollars from sponsors also allow an owner to recruit better talent for every position on his team.

Today's sponsor contracts run between $5 million and $15 million. Are they worth it? You can answer that question: How many drivers and teams do you associate with the products that adorn their cars, clothes, and words in post-race interviews?

Factory Support

Many teams also receive factory help. Ford, Dodge, Pontiac, and Chevrolet all want to see their cars win, so they feel it is in their best interests to help the frontline teams that race their cars. Make no mistake about it, though: Manufacturers contract race teams for exposure. Winning is good exposure. Losing is bad exposure, which means an unhappy sponsor. Unhappy sponsors equal less money. Less money results in diminished success. Racing follows the rules of nature, which dictate that the strong prosper and the weak decline.

Perhaps winning is everything, in this sense, with the seeds of victory planted by high-dollar sponsorships, which are a necessity in today's NASCAR. Once the money is in the bag, though, it's time for the business of racing.

Garage to Glory

The trick is not simply to get enough money to race each Sunday, but rather to turn that green into a black-and-white checkered flag. However, it's not as easy as "Build big engine with big money."

Winston Cup teams and their employees play by the same rules as all businesspeople. Revenue must be acquired, payroll met, and bills paid. Just as money can't buy happiness, money alone cannot win races.

There are and have been plenty of teams that have good sponsors, loads of cash, and a quality driver, yet they still don't win. Felix Sabates owned a multiple-car operation with many talented people and brought many advances (such as opulent shops and transporters) to racing. Felix is a longtime and well-liked member of the racing community. However, he was not successful as an individual owner. When Chip Ganassi bought into his

By the late 1980s, the cars more resembled the modern Winston Cup car but were nowhere near as refined.

operation, though, it wasn't long before the same team was consistently winning and was in the running for the 2002 championship until driver Sterling Marlin got hurt and had to stand down for the last seven races of the year. (Incidentally, the Sabates/Ganassi team accom-

After a brilliant career as a crew chief, Ray Evernham (right) made his debut as a car owner in 2001, when Dodge decided to place their "factory" team in his hands upon its return to Winston Cup racing. Here he talks with driver Ken Schrader.

plished this while switching to Dodge, which was just coming back into the sport.)

What matters more than a team's equipment is understanding how to use and apply the equipment. Winning is a matter of chemistry and momentum. How effectively team members work together has a huge impact on the team's success. How they exchange ideas is a major factor. If disgruntled members spread discontent, it has a detrimental effect on the entire effort. Likewise, positive attitudes rub off. Racers are a funny breed. They can accomplish automotive miracles when they're "on," but not winning can plant some ugly bugs.

A few years back, owner Richard Childress hired crew chief Larry McReynolds away from Robert Yates' team and paired him with driver Dale Earnhardt. The competition trembled when the announcement was made. McReynolds, one of the best-ever crew chiefs, was paired with the circuit's most talented driver. However, the results were surprising. The duo never accomplished much and, after a while, Childress swapped crew chiefs between Earnhardt's number 3 car and Mike Skinner's number 31. Soon Earnhardt was back in the winner's circle.

Another example of chemistry at work was owner Jack Roush's decision to switch the personnel on Mark Martin's number 6 car and on Kurt Busch's number 97 car. Martin was paired with veteran crew chief Jimmy Fennig and had a miserable 2001 season. The younger Busch was paired with Ben Leslie, a relatively young crew chief, and they also achieved mixed results. By the end of the 2001 season, things were going downhill fast. Performance of both teams continued to slide and a once proud and winning race program became just another team in the pack. Then Roush made a dramatic change: He switched the teams and put the veteran crew chief Fennig with the new driver, Busch, and the veteran driver Martin with the

Few owners can match Jack Roush for sheer activity. Even with five teams to oversee, Roush finds time to lobby with NASCAR President Mike Helton and to check that the crash cart is properly outfitted.

A driver's duties have grown from driving the car and turning wrenches to driving the car and accommodating fans, as Ward Burton does here, and pleasing sponsors. Companies that spend $10 million a year for a race team want a good representative behind the wheel.

less experienced crew chief, Leslie. Within six races in the 2002 season, Busch had won his first race and he went on to win several others. Martin went back to victory lane within twelve races and was once again threatening to win a championship. Of course, the tools and equip- ment the racers had been working with had not changed significantly. What had changed was the way that ideas and knowledge were exchanged. Busch, who had much less experience than Martin, was helped by the experience of a master crew chief who had worked with the likes of Dale Earnhardt and Bobby Allison. Martin, on the other hand, responded to the youth and open-mindness of the younger crew chief. All of a sudden, the mix was right and the team was winning.

Maintaining the right mix is very important once you get it. When people wondered why Ricky Rudd left Robert Yates Racing after a successful stint, it was reported that one of his main concerns was that parts of the team would split and the mix of people would change. Situations like these underline the importance of team owners, managers, and crew chiefs utilizing effective management skills. Understanding the science of racing is not enough—everyone involved needs to understand *people*.

Some owners are hands-on, some hands-off, but one fact remains the same: It is the owner's responsibility to bring stability and vision to the team. An owner must be involved with the hard decisions about personnel and must be a liaison between the team and NASCAR and between the team and the sponsor. It is the team manager's responsibility to assist the owner in these roles as needed, and it is also the manager's duty to oversee each of the different areas of the team, racing-related or not. As in any business, the manager must be versed in skills from accounting to safety and from public relations to environmental concerns. The manager also must handle the team's personnel by solving problems and offering praise as needed.

So, who's in charge of the car? In recent years, some teams have added car chiefs, but in most cases, the crew chief is the main man. The race car is his responsibility; thus the employees building them are always under his gaze. Crew chiefs tend to spend their days bouncing around the shop answering questions, giving guidance, and making sure things get done properly. They work with the engine department, the chassis and body fabricators, the suspension experts, and the research and development folks.

In order to optimize the performance of the team, each area of the car has experts. The engine room is filled with skilled machinists and engine builders. The chassis and body area is filled with machinists, master metal fabricators, and welders. There are team members in charge of rear gears, transmissions, brakes, carburetors, suspension, and electronics. Shock absorber technology has become so important that there is usually a team member who does nothing but build and evaluate shocks. It's interesting to note that not all of those who work on the car actually lay their hands on it. Teams now employ engineers, metallurgists, and aerodynamics experts to optimize the design of the car before it is ever built.

All of his helping hands aside, rest assured that when the truck rolls out to the track on Thursday, it is the crew chief who must make sure that everything is ready. We will discuss the crew chief's duties further in chapters 4 and 5, as well as those of the Sunday crew—the driver and the pit crew. For all of the thousands of man-hours of competitive work that goes on before the car ever heads to the track, on Sunday it's in the hands of the driver and pit crew, and no team can win unless they are up to the task. It's also fair to say, though, that a team will never have a chance on Sunday if the guys in the shop didn't do their job.

CHAPTER TWO

TOOLS OF THE TRADE

Over the years, probably the only thing that has changed more than the race cars is the shop. In the early days of NASCAR, cars were prepared in the family garage, or even under a tree in the backyard. When the sport became popular, and it was possible to make a decent living racing, it became more common to see teams with a specialized shop for the race team. These shops, however, were a far cry from the modern race shop. They were often little more than a converted repair shop or service station. Modern Winston Cup operations may encompass 100,000 square feet or more. There are dedicated areas for chassis assembly, body fabrication, general assembly, machining, engine assembly, and diagnostics. To run the business, teams have administrative offices, meeting rooms, and modern amenities for the employees, such as lunchrooms and workout facilities.

The primary activity in the main room is the final assembly of new cars and the refurbishing of cars that have been raced. At any one time, many cars in various stages of completion are in the main room. Work in this area ranges from installing suspensions to outfitting interiors.

Main Work Area

While every shop has its own unique characteristics, most share several common design features. The most obvious is the main work area, which is a large, centrally located room where most of the outfitting is done to the cars. Here, the finishing touches are put on newly built cars, and this is where cars that have already been raced are inspected and refreshed. When a newly constructed race car leaves the chassis and body departments, it is moved to this main area for final assembly. There are many bolt-on items that the crews must mount to the bare-bones car, and this main room is where all of these systems are added until the car is ready to race.

A central fixture on the main shop floor is the surface template, which is a large, level, and flat metal surface. While the concrete floor of the shop may not be level, the surface template

Today's teams typically have a stable of a dozen or more cars in various stages of completion, from newly built cars that have never been on the track, to cars damaged in a previous race that are awaiting repairs. No matter the case, the workload is constant for every team.

One of the key elements of car preparation is the surface plate, which allows the team to place the car on an absolutely flat and level surface. Because the rules are so tight, and the teams build the cars right to the edge of the rules, it is imperative that all measurements on the car be true to eliminate time-consuming delays at the track. Track time is limited during practice, and a team cannot afford to waste it fixing a problem that should not have occurred in the first place.

ensures that a car is on a completely level surface for assembly and inspection. Lifts may be located in the main work area and provide team members easy access to the bottom of the car. Main work areas also feature high ceilings with skylights for additional light. The walls of the main shop are usually lined with toolboxes and workbenches and are often decorated in much the same fashion as the race car itself.

Around the perimeter of the main room are individual work centers that are set up to perform a variety of jobs, from rear-gear assembly to sheet-metal fabrication.

Chassis Building Area

The specialized work required for all race cars carries with it a need for specialized workrooms, such as the chassis area. The chassis

Left: Some teams buy their chassis from a supplier, while others manufacture them in house. Either way, it is the strength of this steel skeleton that protects the driver and makes Winston Cup cars so strong.

Below: The primary operations in building a chassis are to measure, cut, bend, and weld, with many feet of steel tubing comprising the finished chassis. While the tools and materials are relatively low-tech, the actual assembly is quite complicated. Each piece must be made to exact standards if the final product is to be correct, as a chassis flaw can mean a handling problem on the track.

Teams not only have to deal with building new chassis, but they must repair damaged ones as well. It takes a pretty bad wreck to total a Winston Cup car, and, as a result, some pretty major damage can be repaired in the chassis shop. This is usually a matter of replacing the front clip, the rear clip, or both. Once the chassis is repaired, the car is repainted, reassembled, and put back into the fleet.

area looks like a thousand other fabrication shops across America, and while the tools and materials are similar, the end result is exotic.

Steel tubing, the backbone material of Winston Cup cars, is stored on racks in its original long and straight form. It requires many steps to convert this raw material into a Win-

ston Cup chassis, and these chassis-dedicated shops house all the equipment needed to accomplish the task. Most prominent are the building fixtures or "jigs," which are used to hold the pieces of the chassis in place while they are welded together. Jigs help the team produce chassis of exact specifications time after time.

The other equipment in the chassis building area is relatively common. Vertical band saws are used to cut the tubing to size. Once cut, the tubing is bent to shape with a hydraulic-powered tubing bender. This machine has different inserts that allow the builder to apply many different radiuses to the different pieces. The ends of each piece are tightly fit before they are welded into place. When it is finally time for a piece to be permanently fitted, it is welded using a wire-fed welder.

Not all teams build their own chassis, but each is capable of repairing them. No team will run a season without damaging some race cars, and while sometimes cars are a total write-off, many can be fixed to race again.

Body Fabrication Area

Whether it has been purchased from an outside vendor or built in-house, the completed chassis is delivered to the body shop. The body shop is where the miraculous work that makes race cars the special machines they are takes place. Winston Cup car construction is, in a way, a flashback to the early twentieth century, when custom coachbuilders made automobile bodies by hand. With the exception of the hood, roof, and deck lid, which are stock parts supplied by the factory and slightly modified

During construction, bodies are assembled with the car in a controlled position. When putting a suspension under the chassis, the team keeps an eye on the height of the car from the beginning. That way, there are no surprises during final inspection.

The cars are prepared for painting in an area outside of the paint booth. Because of the large amounts of dust generated by all of the sanding, hoods and vents suck as many airborne pollutants out of the shop as possible. Teams use paint booths that contain the spray that does not bond to the car, primarily due to government regulations aimed at keeping the environment clean.

by the teams, the car's body is constructed entirely by hand.

A tour of a body assembly room contains few examples of high-tech equipment. There are no computer-controlled machines in a body assembly room. In essence, the same sheet-metal-forming equipment that has been used by fabricators since the turn of the last century is used today. Teams design patterns that allow the initial sizing to be done quickly. Next, shears and saws are used to cut the sheet metal stock into rough-form shapes. Rollers, English wheels, and forming presses are used to bend the complex compound curves into the body panel. While the equipment is low-tech,

the skills required of the fabricator are tremendous. Once the body panels are fabricated one piece at a time, they are welded together onto the chassis.

Paint Area

The last step for a raw body is the paint booth. Just like any other paint shop, team shops must comply with all local, state, and federal regulations. The primary focuses of these regulations are the painter's safety and environmental protection. Today's paint booths have filter systems that catch the airborne paint and fumes. Painters also wear suits and masks to limit their exposure. Ventilation systems and filters keep dust and any other airborne objects out of the paint booth, so it is a rather pure environment. Computers control the paint booths and its systems, which allows the painter to program a variety of controls. All of this sophistication is what makes the paint jobs on a Winston Cup car as slick as any on the road.

Machining Area

To be successful in today's competitive field, teams must find ways to extract more and more speed from the same parts. To accomplish this, teams spend countless hours working within the rules to improve the performance of each and every component of the car. There are two basic ways to do this: fabricating parts from scratch or modifying off-the-shelf parts. Precise machining facilitates both.

Conventional machines and computer numerically controlled (CNC) machines are the two main types of machining equipment. These machines typically include lathes, mills,

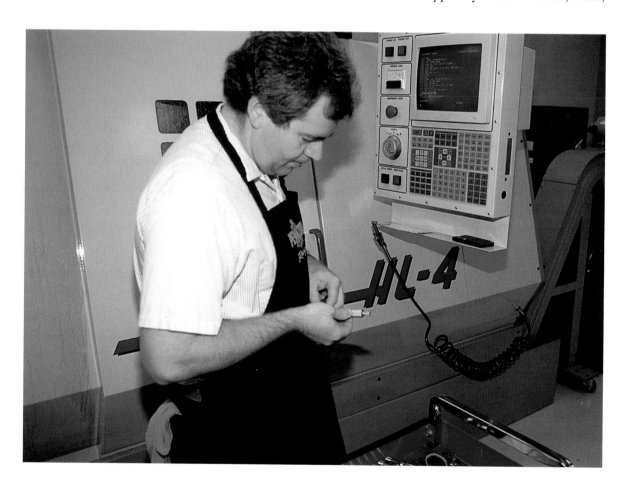

Computer numerically controlled (CNC) machining centers are an expensive proposition. Purchase prices often run into the hundreds of thousands of dollars. However, if they are used properly, they can pay for themselves in short order. A computer controls the tools' movements; thus parts can be made faster and with fewer mistakes.

drill presses, and grinders, and a human operator controls the machines, movements. CNC equipment performs many of the same functions as conventional equipment, but it also offers some big advantages, including speed, accuracy, and the ease with which it can repeat a saved function.

CNC equipment comes in the form of vertical mills (the tool spins along a vertical axis), horizontal mills (the tool spins along a horizontal axis), and CNC lathes (the part spins along a horizontal axis). The drawback of CNC equipment is cost.

To operate CNC equipment, a team member programs the desired movements of the machine and then loads the needed machine tools into the machine's turret. The part that is to be machined is then placed in a fixture that holds the part stable. Once the part is secured in the fixture, the operator begins the machining cycle.

At this point, the machine takes over, and the operator can more or less stand with his hands in his pockets and watch. The machine automatically reads the program, selects the tool, and performs the desired movements. For example, if a part requires four holes of different sizes, the machine drills one size, changes drill bits, drills the next size, changes tools, and so on—all without human assistance.

After programming the machine and loading the appropriate tools, the operator's main function is to load and unload parts, check the accuracy of the machining after a part is finished, and make certain that the tools in the machine are in proper working order. When machining is complete, the program is saved and the same functions can be performed later with minimum setup time.

Outfitting a well-equipped machine shop is expensive. By the time the owner is through writing checks, the sum is most likely stag-

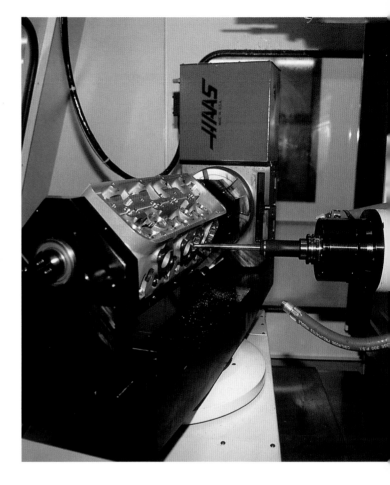

When the CNC machine is in operation, the operator is removed from the action, protected by a sliding door that must be closed before the tool will begin cutting chips. Here, the ports of a cylinder head are being machined. By storing the desired machining commands in a program and using the same fixture to hold the part, many pieces can be machined to very tight tolerances with identical dimensions.

gering. A simple manual mill is by no means cheap, while CNC machine centers cost in the hundreds of thousands of dollars. This price does not include all of the fixtures and tooling required to actually make parts.

Engine Machining Room

Aside from specialty parts, teams spend quite a bit of time refining engine parts for both maintenance purposes and to generate additional horsepower from them. Dedicated machines that are designed to work on specific engine part are essential elements for these tasks. There are individual machines to bore and hone blocks, turn crankshafts, and cut valve seats in heads. Separate work areas are set up for different engine parts, from blocks and heads to smaller parts like connecting rods. To get as much horsepower as possible out of the engines, builders refine each component as much as possible within the rules. Each machine does one thing, and does it well. A quality Winston Cup engine machining room may have upwards of 20 different machining centers. After each individual engine component is crafted, it is moved to the engine room for assembly.

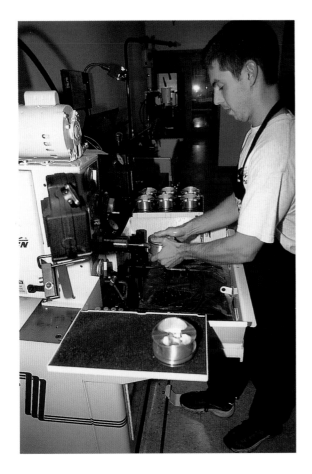

A machinist hones a piston prior to engine assembly.

The engine room is usually the cleanest room in the shop and resembles a laboratory more than a garage. Once all of the machining is complete, the components are brought into this room to be assembled. This is another area of stock-car racing where the tools are relatively simple but the know-how is very complex.

Engine Assembly Area

The engine assembly area is where specialized parts come together to create a high-horsepower engine. This is obviously an area of critical importance. Engine assembly is hands-on work that is facilitated through the use of only basic hand tools.

The first step in the process is to bolt the bare block onto the engine stand. The stand not only holds the block steady, it also allows the builder to rotate the block and lock it into position, and the team members can then work on the top and the bottom of the motor with ease. Blocks and heads are assembled separately, usually by different builders, and are then bolted together as a finished unit. When the engine is complete, it is put into inventory, and another project is begun.

Cleanliness is of paramount importance in an engine room. Contaminants can easily hamper an engine's performance, so everything possible is done to ensure they don't get in. Clean air, clean floors, a clean workbench, clean parts, clean tools, and clean hands are all essential to create a "sterile" environment. A grain of dirt in the wrong spot can take a team out of a race as quickly as a wreck.

Diagnostics

Proper assembly of the engine and chassis doesn't guarantee success. In order for a team to be competitive, it must know the exact specification and condition of each part of the car. This is where the team's diagnostic capabilities come into play.

Aside from a measuring tape, the most common piece of diagnostic equipment is the engine dynamometer (dyno). Each motor built is placed on the dyno, where the power output (torque and horsepower) is monitored and recorded at a wide range of rpm. This shows not only how much power is produced, but

With the elimination of practice motors and qualifying motors, race motors must now last an entire weekend of racing. Many engine builders spend Sunday afternoons at home on the couch watching the race, but their contributions are always present. There is no doubt that a few extra horses help a driver, but if the engine goes up in smoke halfway through the race, it makes for a long Monday. In truth, it is amazing how rarely these 9,000-rpm time bombs fail.

Top: A dyno with an engine ready to evaluate. The engine will run on this stand, just as it runs in the car, as all of the engine's support systems are integrated into the dyno system. Coolant, oil, fuel, and air are all piped into the engine, and, as a result, its operation closely resembles what it will do when it is part of the car. The dyno enables builders to make changes to the engine and immediately find out their impact, as engines can also be run for extended periods to test longevity and reliability.

Above: The dyno control panel is located in an adjoining room. The dyno operator can simulate the different demands placed on the engine by adjusting the amount of resistance.

A relative newcomer to the diagnostic equipment of the teams is the Spintron. An engine is mounted on the Spintron, but it does not run under its own power. Instead, a large electric motor on the Spintron is used to turn the engine to any rpm range the operator desires. While the engine is turning, lasers are used to measure minute movements of the valvetrain, and the information is recorded and charted by a computer.

when it is produced in the powerband. The dyno allows engine builders to see the effects of any changes they have made to the engine, whether it is a different camshaft lift and duration or a new exhaust configuration, and determine these modifications' impact on power.

To use the dyno, the engine is mounted on it, with connections that provide fuel, coolant, and exhaust hooked to the engine. The dyno also has a brake, which provides resistance and simulates the drag an engine will experience during race conditions.

One of the newer engine-diagnostic devices used by Winston Cup teams is the Spintron. This machine measures minute movements

within the valvetrain of the motor as it runs. It's notable that the engine does not *really* run, at least in the conventional sense. Instead of making the engine turn with fuel and fire, the power is supplied through a large electric motor. This motor turns the engine up to any rpm that the engine tester desires. Not only can a tester select a fixed engine speed, he can also program the Spintron to run a pattern that mimics a particular track.

Different tracks place different demands on an engine. At Talladega, a driver never lets off of the throttle as he goes around the track. At Martinsville, however, a driver accelerates at the beginning of the straightaway, deceler-

When you get down to it, the power that matters is the power that is transferred from the rear wheels to the track. Today's teams can measure this by using a chassis dyno. Engine dynos show how much power the engine produces. However, as the power is transferred through the clutch, transmission, drive shaft, and rear end, some power is lost.

ates at the end, and may feather the throttle through the turn. So, when developing an engine for Martinsville, the Spintron can be programmed to accelerate and decelerate the engine along the same pattern the car will see as it rounds the track. In fact, an engine can run an entire simulated race for any track, which will enable the team to measure not only an engine while it is fresh, but also when it is at the end of its projected life.

Many teams also have a chassis dyno. This device measures the horsepower at the wheels, as opposed to at the flywheel. As the power of the motor is transferred through the drive-train, wheel power is lost due to the resistance and friction of the transmission and rear end. The chassis dyno provides the most important horsepower data, which is how much horsepower gets to the wheels and can be applied to the track.

Engines and chassis are not the only parts on a race car that are measured electronically. The size and location of other parts can be measured very accurately using coordinate measuring machines (CMMs). These machines link a measuring probe to a computer and give very accurate dimensional readings. CMMs come in different sizes. Small machines measure smaller parts, anything from a piston to a control arm. By touching different areas of a part with the probe, the exact dimensions of a single part can be measured very accurately to the ten-thousandth of an inch. Large CMMs can be used to measure an entire car. Large CMMs feature an articulating arm that is large enough to reach around the car; thus the entire car (body, suspension, or both) can be measured much more accurately than with a tape measure and calipers. These machines are much more accurate and faster than old measuring methods.

Certain smaller components of the car require their own diagnostic systems. Shock absorbers are a prime example. Shocks have become very important to the handling of the race car. As a result, teams use a shock dyno to measure each shock's performance. Shock dynos measure and record the resistance in both the compression and rebound stroke of the shock absorber. By the time the car is ready to go the track, the team is as confident as possible that each part of the car is in top working order. All in all, just about as much time is spent on inspecting the parts of the car as is spent on assembling them.

Dirty Room

Even while all of this work is going on, one of the goals of every shop manager is to keep the shop as clean as possible, and one of the shop manager's biggest allies in this effort is the "dirty room," where the messiest of tasks are completed. By concentrating the dirtier jobs in one area, the rest of the shop is kept cleaner. Dirty rooms are used for cleaning everything from an entire race car to individual parts. Race cars can get quite dirty during a race, with dust, oil film, and grime the main culprits. If the car takes an off-track adventure, dirt will get in every nook and cranny. Cars also have a tendency to get a good deal of rubber built up on them. Racing tires are much softer than street tires, which is the main reason that they handle so much better. It is also why they do not last very long. As a car races, the abrasive track grinds small pieces of hot, soft rubber off of the tire. Much of this rubber goes onto the track, but a good bit of it gets caked up in the fender wells and in every other imaginable spot under the car. The dirty room is usually the place where a lucky team member gets the glamorous job of scraping the rubber off. Dirty rooms usually

Virtually every part on a Winston Cup car is measured a number of times. One of the newer methods of measuring is the coordinate measuring machine (CMM). These machines come in a variety of sizes, and they link a measuring probe to a computer. The result is a quick, easy, and extremely accurate method of measuring. All the operator has to do is touch the part with the probe, and the exact point of contact is recorded. As the operator touches more critical measuring points, the computer calculates distances and angles between the selected points. Parts that may take hours to inspect with calipers and gauges can be measured more accurately, and in just minutes, using a CMM.

have a pressure washer, a steam cleaner, and a chemical part-washing station. Often, the shop's grinders are located in the dirty room to keep the grinding dust from spreading throughout the shop.

Storage Area

It takes a lot of stuff to keep a Winston Cup team afloat. While a concentration of suppliers near the shop is helpful, each team keeps a large inventory on-site. Obviously, time cannot be wasted running around for parts when the team is trying to get a car ready to go to the track.

Neatness and organization are mandatory in a storage area. Time saved finding a part is time that can be spent working on the race car. Shelf after shelf is filled with every part necessary to build and maintain a fleet of race cars. Some parts, because of their ungainly shapes, must be secured in custom storage devices.

When building a Winston Cup car, teams use three types of parts—factory, aftermarket, and handmade. Factory pieces are few and far between. Parts of the body, the roof, hood, and rear deck lid, are factory "skins." The heads and blocks also come from the factory. That's about it for factory parts for these "stock" cars.

A large number of the parts on a car are aftermarket parts, though only aftermarket parts that conform to NASCAR rules may be used. Ranging from pistons to tachometers, aftermarket parts are specifically engineered for racing by independent companies that are usually not affiliated with an original equipment manufacturer (OEM). These parts' advanced designs provide stronger yet lighter components, which is critical. Teams often put custom touches or modifications on aftermarket parts.

Handmade parts include all of the parts designed, engineered, and built by the teams. The biggest of these is the frame/roll cage and the body. In addition, many other parts of the car, from brackets to suspension components, are built from scratch by the teams. NASCAR watches these modifications closely.

The parts warehouse is another aspect of racing where extraordinary detail benefits a team. Parts must be checked out so a replacement can be purchased. They must properly be checked in so that inventory can be tracked. The total inventory can be of great value, and, like any financial commitment, it must be properly managed. On most teams, this is a full-time job, and having one employee maintain this area offers cost and logistic benefits that far outweigh the cost of this employee's salary.

Shop Surroundings

The outside of the shop is usually decorative in the front and functional in the rear. The fronts of Winston Cup shops vary, though most are beautifully landscaped. Were it not for the signs (and the sound of an engine screaming on the dyno), a pedestrian might mistake the shop for any prosperous service company. Other shops have fronts that resemble a country club or a concert hall. Whether it is acres of manicured lawn, lakes with fountains, or landscaping comparable to Augusta National Golf Club, they incorporate features aimed solely at showmanship. However, these features are not solely eye candy. They can have indirect benefits, such as an aura of pride and creating a favorable impression among sponsors and potential sponsors.

The rear of the shop has a paved area large enough for the car's transporter to maneuver. Often, covered areas are built for the transporter to be stored during the week and during the off-season. In general, there is a storage building or buildings located at the rear of the shop. In these, you'll probably find nonessential items. Racers are human! They tend to keep some things that they don't really need, and in an effort to keep these trinkets and toys from getting in the way of the team's main effort, they often store it out back.

Also behind the shop is the pit crew's practice area, which consists of little more than a replica section of the pit wall. It may be simple, but it is of vast importance. With the cars as equal as they are, track position is more and more critical. Even if a driver has the fastest car on the track, a bad pit stop can move him from first to twentieth. By the time the driver works his way through all of the traffic (if he can, and if he can do it without getting caught up in an accident), he will probably have used up his tires and will no longer be the fastest car. Likewise, there is no better way for a driver to pass than in the pits. With a great pit stop, a driver can go from fifth to first while not using up tires or banging fenders in the process.

Polishing Touches

As racing developed into more of a business than a hobby, owners began to recognize the importance of both mental and physical fitness to their drivers and team members. In short, the professional and polished finish of a shop makes an impact on the spirit. Let's face it. If you work in a dark, dirty, and cramped workplace, you are much more likely to have a dark, dirty, and cramped attitude. The reverse is also true. If you have a well-lit, clean, and spacious work area, it is much easier to keep a good attitude. So, the extra expense of "polishing" a race shop is not *entirely* ego. If it makes for a better attitude, then it is worth it.

In today's shops, you'll usually find a break room that affords team members a place to relax and unwind during breaks and lunch. Another in-house necessity is a weight and workout room. Physical training is now an essential component for success. While there are some engine builders who would probably fall to pieces if they had to run a mile, active crew members recognize that their performance can be greatly enhanced by being as fit as possible. Obviously, it is the pit crew that needs to be in the best shape. Strength, speed,

A modern Winston Cup shop houses a large inventory of parts. In the storage room, shelf after shelf of parts is neatly arranged. This shelf houses shocks, springs, cylinder heads, radiators, hoses, and much more.

and dexterity pay off with shorter pit times. However, the entire team can benefit from being in shape. Running around the garage all weekend and constantly working on a race car is physically demanding. The day starts early at the track. Team members are usually lined up at the garage gate before six in the morning, with wake-up coming before five. Once at the track, there is hard work to be done: pushing the car, jacking up the car, changing parts on the car. Less glamorous work is required, too, such as unloading the transporter and pushing toolboxes, pit carts, and crash carts around the garage area. Team members are constantly going from the transporter to the garage to the pits. They walk on concrete all day, and they seldom get the chance to sit down. They usually leave the track at six or seven in the evening. It's a twelve-hour workday when it's all said and done. The better physical shape the team is in, the better their chances are to survive and thrive each day.

CHAPTER THREE

WINSTON CUP RACE CARS

Winston Cup race cars are some of the most archaic race cars out there. In a day when carbon fiber and titanium have become commonplace, Winston Cup race cars still use steel. They still use carburetors in a fuel-injected world. While on the surface this may seem simplistic, the truth is that the work done by Winston Cup teams is just as detailed and exact as in more exotic forms of racing. In fact, refining this older technology can be more difficult than simply adapting to the latest and greatest innovations, as there are no breakthrough changes available. For the most part, Winston Cup teams constantly improve on the tried and true.

Stock-car racing began with . . . stock cars! The early races were filled with production cars, most of which had completed their civilian lives before being converted to race cars. Now, there are only a few pieces of a Winston Cup car that can be considered stock. Just about every piece of the car is either handmade by the team or bought from an aftermarket supplier that makes dedicated racing components. With so few stock parts on today's race cars, inspectors at the track serve as referees of what's legal. Teams wisely keep the inspection process in mind throughout the building process.

Today's rule book contains tight controls that allow the teams little room for uniqueness in their modifications. Throughout the car, though, they are allowed to make small changes that, when added together, give an edge. The rule book evolves with the times and the latest gimmicks that teams implement. As teams show up at the track with modifications that are not directly disallowed by current rules, the rule book is adjusted. If it's not in the rule book, then it's okay, right? Often, this isn't the case, and the next week's rule book reveals a specific rule prohibiting these latest "innovations."

This pattern has repeated itself week after week for decades, and the result is the much-refined modern Winston Cup race car. When it all started, the cars were truly stock. Over time, they have evolved into hand-built marvels.

From Parts to Race Car

As noted in chapter 2, a Winston Cup car's life begins on the jig, a large fixture on which the frames and roll cages are assembled. This fixture holds the individual pieces of steel tubing during assembly and gives the car builders two

The modern Winston Cup chassis is probably the most graphic example of how much the sport has changed over the last 50 years. While modern chassis provide for better-handling race cars, the greatest benefits are in the area of driver safety.

Four primary parts make up the chassis: the frame rails, the roll cage, the front clip (or subframe), and the rear clip. Here, a roll cage is assembled. It will later be mated to the frame rails.

things that are of critical importance when building any mechanical device: accuracy and repeatability. Accuracy is of obvious importance, as the chassis must not only be to the specifications of the team, but it must also meet the specifications of NASCAR in order to be legal. Repeatability is also important, as the team must know the chassis inside and out if their track notes are to mean anything. Crew chiefs keep extensive notes of all setups that have been run at each track under different conditions. Every adjustment made to the car during practice sessions and races, and the result of each particular adjustment, is noted.

Chassis

There are four main components that make up the chassis: the frame rails, roll cage, front subframe, and rear subframe. When construction of the chassis begins, the first step is to lay the frame rails to create the foundation for the rest of the chassis. The frame rails consist of two side rails made from magnetic-steel box tubing, and they must be built parallel with no offsets. Once the frame rails have been laid, the fabrication of the roll cage begins. The roll cage provides stiffness for the entire car and is the primary contributor to driver safety. Many feet of steel tubing are blended to create a strong roll cage. The brute strength of the roll cage is what prevents injury upon impact.

The assembly of the roll cage starts at the bottom and is built up from the frame rails. Major pieces, such as the main roll bar, are attached to the lower frame first. Connecting pieces are then welded into place between the major structural pieces. The firewall, the floor pan, and the rear wheel wells are about the only sheet-metal pieces added during the construction of the roll cage. The front subframe is the structure that extends from the firewall to the front of the car. Suspension fittings and spring and shock mounts are built into the front subframe, and in order for the finished car to handle properly, all of these must be positioned correctly. A mistake here could mean a handling problem on the track. The rear subframe extends rearward from the back of the main frame rails, up and over the rear axle, and back down to hold the fuel cell. It includes the mounting points for the rear springs, shocks, panhard bar (track bar), sway bar, and fuel cell. Any modifications from the

When the chassis is complete, it is put on rollers and pushed to the body fabrication shop. If everything was done correctly, the body workers have a true foundation on which to hang the body. At this point in the construction process, all cars are pretty much the same. In fact, there is more than one car out there that has changed from Ford to Chevy or from Chevy to Ford and back again.

The same template that the car must fit at the track is used from the beginning of construction.

traditional chassis design must be submitted to the NASCAR series director (in blueprint form) at least 60 days before the car is to compete. If the new design is approved, the competitor must submit the completed frame and chassis for inspection at least 30 days before the car is to compete on the track. Even if NASCAR approves the blueprint, it does not necessarily mean that the completed chassis will be approved. When the chassis is complete, it is ready for the body to be mounted and the other components added.

Each part of the body has particular tasks that it must accomplish and special areas that the team must address. The body contains the only true stock pieces on a stock car. The roof skin, the hood skin, and the rear deck lid skin are all stock pieces. Competitors must use the factory-produced hood for the make and

model car being raced, but the original support panels, used to hold the sheet-metal hood rigid, are again replaced with custom supports. The hoods must also be secured to the roll cage with wire rope to keep them from flying off in an accident.

The air intake for the carburetor is located on the centerline of the car, between the back of the hood and the front of the windshield. A clean hood profile is necessary for good airflow over the car. On longer tracks, if the hood is damaged, the disturbance of this airflow will dramatically slow a race car. Short-track performance is usually not affected by cosmetic hood damage. The front and rear bumpers cover the body of the car and are produced by the manufacturer but approved by NASCAR. These one-piece units are produced for racing purposes only. The dimensions and shape of

When the top, front, and rear are completed, the sides of the car are fabricated. The sides of the car are made in a number of pieces, but when complete, they appear as one piece. Each piece is welded together, ground flush, and smoothed with body filler.

the bumper covers are established before the season begins to ensure that no model gains an unfair advantage by converting the multiple-piece production car's bumper to a one-piece racing unit. This critical piece of the car is one area that NASCAR officials massage in order to create parity between the four models racing.

Openings are cut in the front bumper cover to allow air to be directed to various systems, primarily the brakes and engine, that

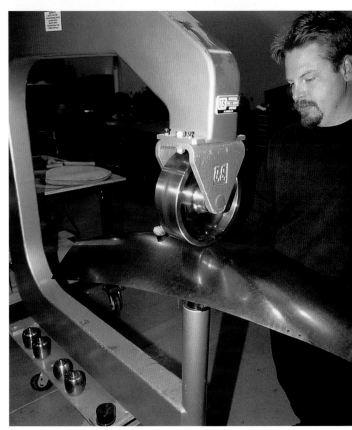

The English wheel is used to roll curves into the sheet metal. It is a simple machine, but operating it correctly takes a great deal of training. The pressure of the steel rollers combined with the fabricator's movement of the sheet metal results in smooth bends in the piece.

46

require cooling. These grille openings are then covered by two layers of wire screen to protect the car from debris. The air dam's purpose is prevent as much air as possible from going under the car. The more air that goes under the car, the more drag and lift the car has. As the car goes faster, the lift increases. If the air dam is damaged, on longer, faster courses the result is a slower car that is more difficult to drive. Stock roof panels for the make and model car being raced are mandatory, and the height, shape, and size of the roof cannot be changed. Airflow over the roof is also of critical importance. How the air flows off the roof, rear window, and deck lid influences the way

the air hits the rear spoiler, which in turn affects the way the car handles. Teams go to great lengths to make sure the airflow to the rear spoiler is optimized while still ensuring that the roof profile remains legal. Deck lids (or trunk lids) retain their stock shape, contours, and appearance. When closed, they are held shut with pin fasteners, and they must have working hinges and a device to keep the lid up when it is open. The deck lid is also tethered to the roll bar with cables to prevent it from flying off during a crash. Rear spoilers, mounted at the rear of the deck lid, are nonadjustable. In an effort to balance the downforce and aerodynamic efficiency of each model of car being raced,

After the body is assembled, it is sent to the paint booth for a coat of primer. If it is not painted, the steel body will quickly rust. Most of the final assembly takes place while the car is in this state. Often, cars are taken to the track and tested before the final paint job is applied.

NASCAR may mandate different spoiler widths and heights for each model.

Winston Cup cars have no doors, though the sides of the car must maintain the factory contours and accent lines. The sides of the car are made of sheet-metal pieces that are riveted and welded into place, with all weld seams smoothed out. As with all other body pieces on the car, great care is taken to produce the pieces to exacting tolerances. This is more easily said than done, considering the compound curves in the body of a Winston Cup car. When measuring lap speeds down to one-hundredth or one-thousandth of a second, the slightest flaw can upset the aerodynamics of the car and slow it down or affect the handling.

Painting the Car

When "hanging the body" onto the chassis is complete and all of the weld seams and other irregularities are smoothed out, it's time to paint the car. First, primer is applied. Often, after the primer coat has been applied, the car is returned to the main shop so that assembly can be completed before the final color coat is put on the car. This is to prevent the paint from being scratched by team members during assembly. In fact, cars are often tested in

After painting, the interior is outfitted. All of the roll bars within the driver's reach are padded for protection during accidents.

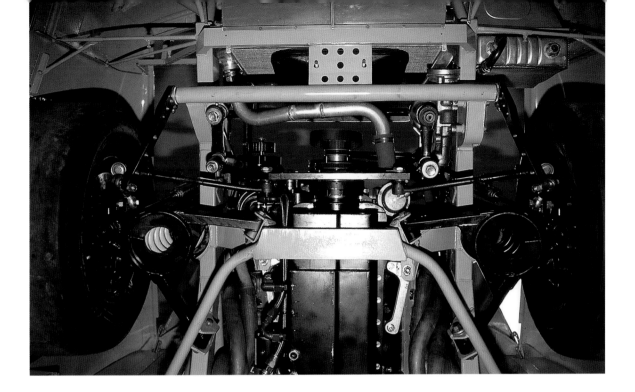

The front suspension as viewed from under the car. The lower control arms, which incorporate the lower spring mounts, are clearly visible. The springs can be seen above them (one is yellow and one is blue). The steering center link and tie rods can be seen running from steering knuckle to steering knuckle.

primer and are not painted until the car is ready for actual competition.

Most teams use a base coat/clear coat system for the final paint job, just like production cars. Once the paint has dried, the team applies the stickers. The stylish graphics you see on the cars are usually stickers, which are much less expensive and time-consuming to apply than custom paint. The rule book governs some decals, such as the car's numbers. Numbers must be at least 18 inches high and located under the door window and on the roof.

Bolt-Ons

Once the body is complete and the interior painted, it is time to add the bolt-on systems to the car. This is a time-consuming process. While a race car's interior is much less detailed

than a production model's, there is work that needs to be done in this area, with safety and driver comfort the main priorities. The dashboard is fabricated out of magnetic steel and must be welded into place. All gauges and controls must be positioned so that the driver can use them with minimal distraction. Gauges are usually mounted so that when all of the needles are pointing straight up, everything is okay. Different drivers like their gauges arranged differently, however.

Teams use wink-type three-dimensional rearview mirrors with a maximum width of 26 inches, and the rearview mirror may not extend outside the car. The seat in a Winston Cup car is custom-fit to suit the preference and size of each driver. While a driver's height and weight impact the building of the seat, the

The front coil spring is installed between the lower mount, located on the lower control arm, and the upper mount, located on the frame rail. The top mount, shown here, is attached to a threaded bolt, often called a jack bolt, and runs through a threaded fitting in the frame. Once the spring is installed and the bolt is tightened, the spring is compressed. If the bolt is loosened, the spring will be allowed to expand. This is known as adjusting wedge, and it gives the team a method of changing the weight distribution of the car without changing the springs.

preferred driving positions of drivers vary greatly. Some like to sit close to the steering wheel, others farther away. Some sit as low as possible in the car, while others like to be more elevated. Each time a car has a new driver, it is reseated. The accelerator, brake, and clutch pedal location are commonly driver-specific in their location, too, so they are changed with each new driver.

Two ignition systems are mounted to the right of the driver, a primary ignition and a backup system. These are mounted in the cockpit in order to shield them from both heat and debris, and the activators for each must be within easy reach of the driver.

While padded roll bars will help the driver avoid injury in a crash, a complete fire-extinguishing system helps protect the driver in the event of fire. Insulating pads are installed along the firewall and floorboard to help protect the driver from the car's heat. A two-way radio, activated by a button on the steering wheel, is also installed.

While the setup is different, the rear suspension works much like the front suspension. The rear suspension of a Winston Cup car uses coil springs, as does the front. However, instead of using short control arms like the front suspension, the rear uses long trailing arms.

All cars must use windshields made of 1/4 inch-thick, hard-coated polycarbonate material, and a minimum of three metal braces must be used to support the windshield from the inside of the car. On tracks shorter than 1-1/2 miles and on road courses, the passenger side window (or door window) must be removed. A nylon web screen is installed in the driver's side-door window opening. These screens are made of nylon mesh, with each strip being a minimum of 3/4 inch and a maximum of 1 inch wide. The minimum screen size is 22 inches wide by 16 inches tall.

At this point in the construction, the basic shell of the car is complete, and the next step is bolting the suspension under the car. There are few things in Winston Cup racing as important as a properly tuned suspension (discussed further in chapters 4 and 5). Winston Cup cars have a very traditional (some say antiquated) suspension design. With a solid rear axle and coil spring/shock setup on both front and rear, the general design bears more similarities with a modern pickup truck suspension than with the modern front-wheel drive, independent suspension, MacPherson strut designs on passenger cars.

Suspension

The front of the chassis is linked to the suspension by control arms (or "A" frames). The insides of the control arms are mounted to the frame and pivot on mounts with heavy-duty bushings. On the outside, they are attached to the steering knuckles using ball joints. The front coil spring's lower mount is on the lower control arm. Winston Cup cars use specially manufactured tubular control arms, which are much lighter and stronger than their stock counterparts.

In the rear, trailing arms link the chassis and the rear suspension. The fronts of the trailing arms attach to the body with hinged fixtures just aft of the center of the car. The ends of the trailing arms attach to the rear axle and have fixtures that connect the rear shock absorbers and the rear springs, which are mounted between the trailing arms and the frame.

Winston Cup cars use heavy-duty steel coil springs on both the front and rear suspensions. The front springs mount between the lower control arm (on the bottom) and the frame (on the top). Rear springs must also be made of heavy-duty magnetic steel with both ends closed. On the rear suspension, the upper and lower coil spring mounts must be located between the rear frame side rails. The rear lower mounts must be located on either the rear axle trailing arms or on top of the rear axle housing. Winston Cup cars use heavy-duty shocks, similar to the original shocks on the models being raced. Although they are aftermarket racing shocks, any shock used must be available to all competitors.

Sway bars are another link between chassis and suspension. They are mounted to the underside of the body and the ends are connected to the lower control arms on the front and the trailing arms on the rear. The stiffer the sway bar, the tighter the link between the chassis and the suspension. The tighter the link, the less movement between the suspension and the chassis, which results in less body roll when the car is turning. There is a wide range of sway bar strengths available, so teams can tune the body roll to fit the track being raced.

The track bar, another rear suspension piece, is used to keep the rear end square under the car. As the car goes through the turn, the rear end twists in relation to the body. Track bars are attached to the frame at one end and to the end of one of the trailing arms at the other end. Usually, the bar runs from the left side of the body to the right-rear trailing arm.

Braking importance varies from race to race. At big tracks, brakes are of little importance and seldom fail. At short tracks, they are as important as horsepower, and can get so hot they can melt a tire. The quickest way to see how important brakes are at any one track is to monitor how much effort teams make to keep them cool. This car is headed for a short track, which is evident by the three cooling hoses ducted to the left front brake. At a superspeedway, the thick pads and rotors of the short track are abandoned in an effort to save weight. Everything is lighter, including the rotors, which are thinner and may have holes drilled in them. The only reason that this is possible is because at tracks like Talladega, the main purpose of the brakes is to slow and stop the car for servicing during a pit stop.

This extra support is critical for stability through the turns. The track bar may be adjusted to refine the handling of the car during both practice and the race.

Steering and Braking
Steering is pretty straightforward, with an old-fashioned worm-type gear system assisted by a power-steering pump.

Braking capabilities vary, depending on which variety of Winston Cup track a car is built for, but all brake systems are four-wheel disc with multipiston calipers. The master cylinders are a non–power-assisted type. Brake pads are made especially for the purpose of racing. The extreme heat encountered by race brakes would wear out normal street pads far too quickly. Instead of being made predominantly of an organic material, racing pads are a carbon and metal mix, which is much more heat- and wear-resistant. On many tracks, slowing down is as important as speeding up.

Every week, the team turns out motors for the next race. While teams may take three engines to the track, they are not allowed to change once practice has begun. If they do, they will lose their qualifying position and have to start the race from the rear.

Engines

A car that handles in the turns is a wonderful thing for a driver and necessary for success, but a car that excels down the straightaway is mighty nice too. You can't win on horsepower alone, but a little extra horsepower is always welcome. Again, by modern automotive standards, Winston Cup engines are very old-fashioned. In a world of electronic engine management and fuel injection, Winston Cup cars rumble along with carburetors and distributors. Only small-block V-8 engines are allowed with a maximum compression of 12:1 in any cylinder. Each car must run the engine of its make, meaning you can't put a Ford engine in a Chevrolet body. The racing divisions of Dodge, General Motors, and Ford manufacture the blocks specifically for racing.

The cast-iron racing blocks (aluminum blocks are prohibited) differ from the production blocks in that they have thicker cylinder walls to eliminate distortion and give a better surface for the rings. Improved water passages increase the cooling ability, and the additional bulkhead material built into the main bearing bosses better secures the crankshaft, which is held in place with four-bolt main bearing caps. Increased strength around the deck surface, where the heads bolt onto, increases engine stability. Teams can work on the blocks, but they can't change the material, the number of cylinders, the angle of cylinders, the number and type of main bearings, the location of the camshaft, or the overall configuration.

The power of the motor is collected and transmitted by the crankshaft. The crankshaft bears the brunt of the force of the combustion in the cylinder, turning the downward motion of the piston into a rotary motion (with the help of the connecting rods), and provides the momentum to push the piston back to the cylinder head for the next go-around. The crankshaft lobes are tapered on the leading edges to reduce windage (drag created by the front edge of the crankshaft lobes passing through the air and oil in the block), allowing the engine to spin easier and increasing horsepower and response.

Connecting rods—only solid magnetic steel connecting rods are allowed—connect the piston to the crankshaft. Most are forged, H-beam-style rods that are heavy and very strong. Engine builders tend not to give up much on the rods, not wanting to risk strength for a small performance gain. Engine builders may use any type of round aluminum piston, but they may not weigh less than 400 grams. Pistons take an incredible pounding during practice, qualifying, and 500 miles of racing. With the high compression and intense combustion pressures experienced in a racing engine, pistons occasionally fail, usually burn-

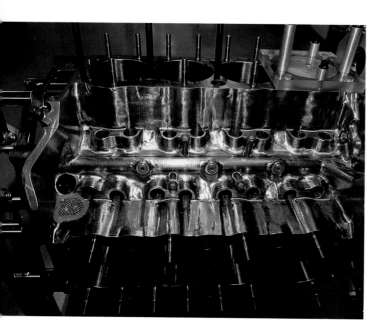

The top of the block, which offers a view of the lifter bores. Note the polishing to improve oil flow.

ing a hole through the top of the piston (also known as holing or burning a piston).

In any motor, pistons perform two tasks. When moving downward in the cylinder on the power stroke, they transmit the energy of the combustion to the crankshaft. They behave much as a bullet does when moving down the barrel of a gun as a result of the hot, expanding gas of the ignited gunpowder. Unlike a bullet, the piston has to change direction at the end of the barrel and move back the other way. When the piston moves upward on the exhaust stroke, it forces the spent gases out of the exhaust port in the cylinder head. The fuel–air mixture enters, and the exhaust gases exit the cylinder by way of the cylinder head. All Winston

Cup cylinder heads are aluminum; however, rules limit each manufacturer to one head design. Teams may not change the material, the number of valves per cylinder, the type of combustion chamber, the location of the spark plugs, the orientation of the spark plugs, the arrangement of the valves, the type of valve actuation, the valve actuation in relation to the cylinder, the angle of the valves, the number of intake ports, the number of exhaust ports, the center distances of the intake ports referenced to the cylinder bore, the center distances of exhaust ports referenced to the cylinder bore, the shape of the ports at the mating surface of the manifolds, the shape of the intake and exhaust ports at the mating faces of the

Once the bottom end of the motor is assembled, the cylinder heads are bolted on. Shown is the bottom of a cylinder head, which offers a look at the combustion chamber and the valve seats. These seats ensure a tight fit when the valve is in the closed position.

manifold, the angle of the port face relative to the mating surface of the head to the block, or the firing order.

The valvetrain, which is located on the head, is controlled by the cam. As the cam rotates (getting its power from the crankshaft by means of the timing chain), the lobes on its surface act with the lifters, pushrods, and rocker arms to open and close the valve. The distance the lifter and pushrod move is known as lift, and the time the valve stays open is the duration. Lift is measured in inches (a .600-lift cam has a lobe height of .600 inches), and duration is measured in degrees (a 270-degree cam holds the valve open for 270 degrees of its rotation). Different lifts and durations can dra-

matically change the powerband of an engine. The quicker the valve opens and the longer it stays open, the more intake, exhaust, and power. However, the quicker the valve opens and the longer it stays open also creates a higher angle on the lobe and a greater chance of failure. As a result, engine builders must seek a cam that strikes a balance between durability and an acceptable amount of power.

A camshaft has to be many things. It has to be hard in the lobe area for resistance to friction, but soft enough to flex a little (but not be brittle, which may cause the camshaft to crack and then and break completely). The metallurgy required to do all this is very complex. The lifters ride in cylinders located on the top

Once the cylinder heads are bolted on (with the valves and valve springs already installed), the rest of the valvetrain is assembled.

of the block. The bottom of the lifter sits on the camshaft lobes, transferring the lift of the lobe (through the pushrod) to the rocker arm. Only solid magnetic steel or steel-hydraulic, flat-tappet, barrel-type lifters are allowed. Pushrods are a high-quality racing type, able to withstand the tremendous forces within the valvetrain. These, too, must be magnetic steel. Guide plates are allowed to help support the pushrods. The rocker arms transfer the upward movement of the pushrod into a downward movement, providing the energy to open the valves. Teams use roller-bearing rocker arms of a split-shaft design, which are much stronger than production rocker arms. Unlike many stock rocker arms, these have a roller tip that eliminates friction at high rpm. The valves are the "doors" to the individual cylinders through which only fuel–air mixture and exhaust should flow. Only magnetic-steel and titanium valves are allowed in Winston Cup racing, and there is no restriction on either intake or exhaust valve size. However, the valve location and the valve angle must remain stock.

As a practical matter, the specification of a legal cylinder head dictates the maximum size of the valve seats. There is little room to increase the valve size within these parameters. A maximum of two valves per cylinder is allowed. Valve springs hold the valve closed when it is not being forced open by the rocker arm. They are made from high-quality magnetic steel and, as engine speeds have increased, valve springs have become difficult parts to manufacture. Winston Cup engine speeds have increased to the point where turning over 9,000 rpm is common.

Harmonic problems at a particular rpm cause many valvetrain problems. Staying at an engine speed where bad harmonics occur will increase the chances of engine failure. This is especially a problem at longer tracks, where engines run a long time in one rpm range. Engine builders try to predict the point of bad harmonics and design the engine so that these areas are in an rpm range that is not sustained. Thus, as the engine accelerates or decelerates through this range, harmonics are usually not a problem.

The fuel–air mixture that ultimately flows through the intake valves begins with the air picked up through the intake at the rear of the hood. Once the air has been filtered, it enters the carburetor, where it is mixed with fuel. Winston Cup cars run four-barrel, mechanically advanced, secondary venturi carburetors. Some polishing and other minor internal changes are allowed, but no external alterations are allowed. When the fuel–air mixture exits the carburetor, it flows through the intake manifold to the cylinder head. High-performance aluminum intake manifolds are used, but the manifold used must be a model that has been approved by NASCAR officials. Epoxy fillers may be added to the individual runners to change the flow characteristics of the manifold, but fillers may not be added to the plenum floor or walls.

Once the fuel–air mixture has been burned, the remains flow from the cylinder, through the exhaust port, then to the exhaust system. The exhaust system is made up of three main components: the headers, the collector pipe, and the exhaust pipes. Headers are made from pipe that is bent to a custom fit and run from the exhaust port on the cylinder head to the collector pipe. By making each individual piece the same length, the exhaust system will help pull the exhaust gases from the cylinder, increasing engine efficiency. The shape, lengths, and configuration of the header pipes can be adjusted to tune the powerband of the engine. This allows an engine builder to tailor

Unlike a production engine, where the oil system is contained within the engine, a Winston Cup car has oil moving throughout the car. The high-volume pump moves the oil through an oil cooler, which is a small radiator located behind the left front fender, and through an oil reservoir tank located behind the driver. This system allows the teams to run more oil in the system and keep the engine cooler.

the car's powerband to each track and build the maximum power where it is needed the most.

To supply fuel to the engine, Winston Cup cars use mechanical fuel pumps. Mechanical pumps get their pumping energy from a pushrod actuated by a lobe on the camshaft. For safety reasons, electronic fuel pumps are not allowed in Winston Cup racing. If an engine with a mechanical pump quits running, the fuel quits pumping. However, in a car with an electronic fuel pump, the fuel may keep pumping even if the engine quits running. In a crash situation, this could be disastrous. Instead of a regular production

gas tank, Winston Cup cars are required to use a fuel cell. Fuel cells have a plastic body that is much stronger than a stock tank and much harder to damage.

Electronic ignition systems are used in Winston Cup racing; however, computerized systems are not allowed. The major ignition system components are located in the cockpit, to the right of the driver, in order to protect the components from debris and heat. All cars have two separate ignition systems (two electronic ignition controls and two coils that are mounted side by side in the cockpit). In the event of an ignition failure, the driver can

The clutch is the link between the engine and the drivetrain. Most stock clutches will only have one disc. Winston Cup cars run a three- or four-disc clutch. This provides more disc surface, which increases the clutch's grip. Aftermarket four-speed transmissions are used in all of the cars and, with the exception of road courses and Pocono, drivers usually only shift when exiting the pits. On oval tracks, the cars are geared so that they can stay in fourth gear all of the way around the track.

quickly flip a switch to change to the backup system without having to make a pit stop.

Distributors are mounted in the stock location and maintain the firing order specified by the manufacturer. High-quality aftermarket distributors and heavy-duty plug wires are used. All cars have an alternator and a standard, high-quality, 12-volt automotive battery is used.

Keeping a Winston Cup engine cool is a bit more complicated than keeping a production engine cool. Winston Cup cars run a dry

sump oil system, which is not found on production vehicles. Instead of the oil flowing down to the pan to be recycled through the engine by a pump that picks up the oil from the bottom of the oil pan, the dry sump systems keep the oil in motion at all times. The pump is mounted on the outside of the engine (much the same as an alternator is mounted) and is driven by a belt. After the oil runs through the engine, it is quickly picked up from the bottom of the oil pan and pumped back into the oil

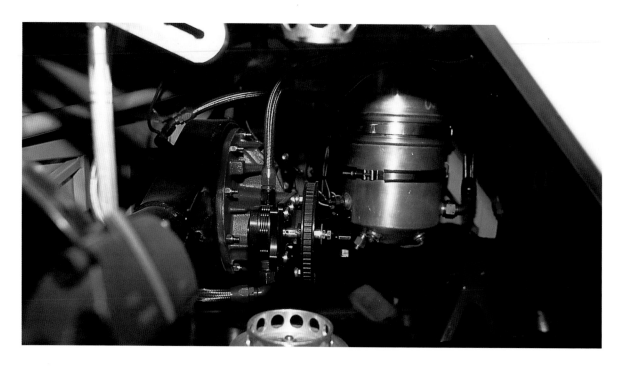

Rear axles are refurbished after every race. Note the pump assembly used to circulate the oil through the rear gear. This keeps the gear cooler and greatly reduces the chance of failure.

system. During circulation, the oil passes through many feet of hose, an oil tank mounted in the left rear of the car, and an oil cooler, which is a radiator used to keep engine oil cool.

The water-cooling systems are similar to their production counterparts, with a few modifications. No special systems that use ice, Freon, or any other coolant can be used. Winston Cup cars all use aluminum radiators that are stock in appearance and mounted in the stock position, not to exceed two inches from vertical. Dust screens are fabricated to prevent debris from entering the radiator. Teams may use either engine-mounted fans or electric fans. If engine-driven, the fan must be steel with no fewer than four blades.

Power from the engine is transferred by the flywheel, which is located at the rear of

the engine and bolted to the crankshaft. The flywheel (which must be solid and made of steel) holds the inertia of the engine and keeps it spinning once the rpms rise. The clutch transmits the power from the engine to the drivetrain. Discs ride against the flywheel to pick up power that is transmitted to the input shaft of the transmission. Multiple-disc clutches are permitted in Winston Cup racing, and the pressure plates and discs must be steel. The minimum clutch diameter allowed is 7-1/4 inches, and most teams use a three- or four-disc system with small-diameter discs. Even though the discs are smaller than those in stock clutches, these multidisc clutches have much more surface area; thus, they will stand up to the extreme strains of a 750-horsepower engine.

When all of the components are installed, the team begins to prepare the car for the race. Throughout this process, many measurements are made to refine the positioning and attitude of the car.

Transmissions

Winston Cup cars use special, aftermarket four-speed transmissions. All forward and reverse gears must be operational. Drive shafts are similar in design to standard production types and must be painted white so that if the brackets fail, the drive shaft can be seen lying on the track. Different tracks require different rear-end gear ratios to ensure that all of the engine power available is optimized. An example of a rear gear ratio is 4.11:1. This means that the drive shaft turns 4.11 revolutions for every 1 revolution of the tire.

To the Track!

When the teams have finished installing all of this equipment, it is time to load the car up and go racing. The teams will make changes to virtually every area of the body, suspension, and engine depending on where the team is racing. As a result, teams will build many different types of cars throughout the season.

CHAPTER FOUR
IN THE GARAGE

W hat you see on the track is only a small portion of Winston Cup racing. While in the end, race day is what it is all about, thousands of man-hours, endless experimentation, and constant analysis take place before the car ever sees the competitive racetrack.

During the weeks and months leading up to a race, the team prepares the car in the shop. Then, days before the race, usually on Thursday, the transporter is packed and rolled out of the shop. A select few team members head to the track for the event, but many more members stay home to prepare for the next week's race.

While hopes are high, tensions are higher. The cost of failure is significant. Working on a race crew is a pressure-filled existence. There is seldom any special recognition when the job is done right, but if something goes wrong, the spotlight is certain to be blinding.

As the sun rises, teams unload their transporters. The car, the tools, and the parts must all be unloaded before the team can get to work tuning the car.

Transporters

A tour through a Winston Cup garage shows that the tractors used by the top teams reflect the cutting-edge technology of today's modern long-haul tractors. They also sport some of the best and most outlandish paint jobs ever seen on commercial trucks. You'll find all of the major manufacturers of long-haul tractors in the garage area of a Winston Cup event: Ford, Freightliner, Kenworth, Mack, Peterbilt, and Volvo. The type of race car a team runs may determine the type of tractor that pulls the transporter to the race. While there are differences between tractors of different makes, most are quite similar. They are usually agile with sharp turning radiuses. On some trucks, the front wheels can turn up to 45 degrees for superb close-quarter maneuvering. All eight of the rear wheels are drive wheels, as the driveshaft supplies power to two differentials, one on each axle. Horsepower and torque numbers vary, depending on manufacturer and engine models; however, most will produce 400 to 500 brake horsepower with 1,500 to 1,700 foot-pounds of torque. The tractors pull the transporters, which teams order with the interior configured the way they want it.

While the top teams may buy new transporters every couple of years, other teams get by using trailers bought from the top teams. New trailers come with the necessary cabinets and drawers, and most of the electrical system is completely fitted. However, there is a great deal of customizing work to be done before the team can head to the track. Usually, the first order of business is to paint both the transporter and the tractor. It is both the practical advertising side and the first-class image side of racing that lead to the incredible paint jobs on today's rigs. The tractor and trailer are highly visible and are the biggest thing that a sponsor can paint. As a result, many of the paint and decal jobs on the trailers are the best you'll ever see.

The large amount of equipment needed at the track means that a great deal of thought is put into the design and layout of a Winston Cup transporter. The floors of the transporters are built differently than standard trailers. They are dropped floors, meaning that they are built much lower to the ground. This increases the cubic volume of space available by exploiting an area that is normally ignored in standard over-the-road trailers. While this dropped-floor design aids capacity, it does have some drawbacks. By completely encasing the rear wheels, it is more difficult to cool them, and this can mean tire or bearing problems due to heat buildup. Teams often fabricate air ducts to feed cool air to these areas to help prevent overheating.

The typical Winston Cup transporter is divided into three main compartments: the lounge (located in the front of the trailer), the car area (located in the top of the trailer), and the main compartment (everything else). The car-storage area is basically a shelf that runs from the back door of the transporter up to the lounge. Within it is room to secure both the primary and backup cars plus a few parts. The cars are loaded using a ramp on the back of the trailer. When the transporter is on the road, the ramp is folded flat against the back of the truck. When the loading ramp is lowered, the car is rolled on, raised to the level of the car-storage compartment, and then rolled in and secured. The ramp is also used to load and unload heavy equipment into the main compartment of the transporter.

No space is wasted, and even the top of the car-storage area (the roof of the transporter) has more than one function. One, of course, is that it serves as a roof, but it also serves as a viewing platform for the team. As a result, it has built-in safety rails. The main compartment is used for storage, a work space, a kitchen, and a place to "hide." At the track, team members may use this area to meet and discuss strategy, cool off in the air conditioning, get out of the hustle and bustle of the garage area, or grab a meal.

The traditional layout has an aisle running down the center of the transporter, with storage compartments and work space located along each side. The floor of the aisle is padded with rubber mats to ease the stress of standing or walking on it all day. The aisle may be offset to allow for deeper cabinets on one side. While all trailers differ somewhat, the typical layout has storage cabinets toward the front of the main compartment. A kitchen and workbench are usually located on the left side of the trailer, while more storage compartments fill the right side. Storage comes in the form of cabinets, bins, and drawers. Each of these is usually labeled to quickly locate whatever may be needed.

Even though it is the smallest part of the trailer and little physical work is done there, the lounge is a very important place. More racing deals are discussed and made in the lounges of transporters than anywhere else. The lounge is also shelter from the storm. Drivers and crews are great with fans and the press, but you have to keep in mind that the teams and drivers are working under a great deal of pressure. Failure at the track can mean job loss or physical harm to drivers and crew. This makes it difficult for all crew members, especially drivers and crew chiefs, to be amiable public figures all of the time. Ironically, the better you run, the more intense things get. When in a championship battle toward the end of a season, the crew chief and driver will have to endure more and more interviews, which means their garage stall and transporter will be crowded with fans and press. When a team has its dreams and car destroyed by an accident or a mechanical failure, within minutes a driver or crew chief will likely have an interviewer asking questions. This is why you often see drivers and crew retreat to the transporter, where they

An army travels on its stomach, and Winston Cup teams are no different. Instead of relying on the concession stand for food, teams have a dedicated cook and all of the equipment to prepare a tasty breakfast, lunch, and dinner.

The main toolbox is one of the first items unloaded, and it is pushed to the garage stall. Toolboxes contain enough hand tools so that time is not wasted waiting for someone else to finish with a wrench.

can collect their thoughts and tempers before facing the public.

It is up to the team to properly load the transporter, and it is up to the truck driver to get it to the track. Often, the truck driver is appointed as the loadmaster and is responsible for making sure that everything is in its place. During the season, it is the same routine week in and week out. After a Sunday race, the truck driver leaves the track and heads to the shop. Obviously, the location of the race dictates when the truck gets back to the shop. If the race is nearby, the trip may be

only a few miles, and the truck will be back to the shop Sunday evening.

A team must also be mindful of the weight and composition of the cargo when loading the truck. The truck must stay under the U.S. Department of Transportation's legal weight limit for commercial trucks. In order to pass through the weigh stations on the highways and interstates, a truck's gross weight cannot exceed 80,000 pounds. Teams are often so close to this weight limit when the transporter leaves the shop that the truck driver can only fill the fuel tanks half full. Though this means

Only after the tools and car have been pushed to the garage stall will the team get to work preparing the car for qualifying practice.

more stops for fuel, the team will be able to carry more gear.

Loads vary depending on the type of track a race will be held on. The load that will be carried to a short track will be quite different from one carried to a superspeed-way. Engines, transmissions, rear gears (different ratios), brakes (heavier for short tracks), and coil springs have different requirements depending on the track. Some items, such as passenger windows and roof flaps, are used on a superspeedway but not on a short track, while heavy brake ducting will be used at short tracks but not on the longer ones.

The team meets up with the truck driver at the track, usually early Friday morning. On a typical race weekend, the transporter pulls into the track before daybreak. At the track, the truck driver receives the parking location, which is based on the point standings, from the NASCAR officials.

As soon as the gate is opened on Friday morning, usually at about six, the team members head to the garage area. Then the unloading begins.

Before the center aisle of the transporter can be accessed, the toolbox, pit cart, and crash cart must be unloaded. The pit and crash carts are not used until race day, so they are stored somewhere in the garage area. The toolbox is rolled to the garage stall to await the race car. These large, rolling units, which are stored in the center aisle of the transporter during transit, are the team's primary mobile tool and parts source.

The primary race car is quickly unloaded so that preparations can begin. The backup car cannot be unloaded unless it is to be used in place of the primary car, as a team is not

Perhaps the biggest winner every race weekend is Goodyear. Teams buy their tires from Goodyear at the track, and Goodyear employees mount them.

During practice, cars make frequent trips to the garage for both engine and suspension adjustments.

allowed to switch back and forth between cars. If the backup car is brought out, it is almost always due to the primary car being wrecked in qualifying or practice. However, on occasion, a team's primary car handles so badly that the crew will test the backup to see if it is any more competitive.

The rims are also unloaded in short order. Teams do not bring tires to the track. Instead, Goodyear sells and mounts the tires at the track in its mounting and balancing facility. At that point, the tires are brought back to the hauler and are usually stacked outside of the trailer.

Next off of the transporter is the team's large amount of miscellaneous gear necessary for race weekend. The transporter is so crammed full of stuff, from gas cans to coolers, that for the trailer to be accessible, all of this gear must be cleared out and put elsewhere. As some team members begin to get the race car ready, others continue to manage the load. As the interior of the transporter empties, the garage stall and area behind and to the sides of the transporter fills up. Only after all of this initial unloading can the team begin to use the transporter as a work area.

At short tracks like Bristol, the infield is not large enough to have a garage, so the teams are forced to work under the sky, rain or shine.

The race cars leave the shop and head to the track already equipped with the team's best engine and handling package for the race. This prepreparation allows the team to get the car on the track with a minimal amount of initial effort. However, it is a rare event when the setup is perfect coming off of the truck. Almost invariably, adjustments must be made. The suspension of the race car is the main thing that is changed when the team is searching for a setup, with the team focused primarily on the spring rates and shock settings. A wide variety of suspension parts are carried to the track in the transporter.

The setup of a race car is almost infinitely adjustable, and for a team to successfully adjust the car, it must have as many options as possible. As well as suspension parts, a team must also have chassis and body materials in case of damage. If the primary car is slightly damaged during practice, the crew may elect to repair it instead of bringing out the backup car. This means that welders, tubing, sheet metal, and fabrication tools must be brought. It is not uncommon for teams to fix bent tubing in the chassis and roll cage or to hang a new fender or quarter panel on the car. Extra front and rear fascia pieces, windshields, windows, hoods, deck lids, and spoilers must also be on hand. Spare engines are also brought. However, the penalty for installing a spare engine is being forced to start in the back of

Alignment and weight distribution are too critical to be left to chance. Teams bring alignment machines and mobile scales to see the results of their adjustments.

the field, so spare engines are not used unless absolutely necessary.

Monday through Thursday, the teams have the luxury of working in shops that feature every kind of automotive machining, fabrication, and testing equipment that is on the market. On the weekends, however, when the effort shifts to the track, the environment is very close to what it was 40 years ago: The team members who work on the race car are sprawled on the ground, wrenches in hand.

Race weekends will find teams working in and around the transporter, in the track's garage area during qualifying and practice,

Before qualifying practice, teams put their cars through the inspection process to make certain that the car is legal. Since teams make continuous changes, cars usually go through the inspection process a number of times.

Teams that have a problem fitting the inspection templates are forced to do a little at-the-track bodywork. When complete, they return to the inspection area before heading out onto the track.

and on pit road during the race. Once the transporter has been parked on Friday morning, it is the center of operations, with the heavy work taking place in the track's garage area. Most garages are designed in such a way that when the rigs are parked, the back of the transporter is almost directly across from the garage stall. This enables the crews to quickly access the parts and equipment that are stored in the transporter.

Garage Work

Once a team is assigned a garage stall, setup begins. The first thing that the teams put in this area is their large roll-around toolbox, which contains all of the hand tools that the team will need. This is where the run-of-the-mill tools are kept. From wrenches to screw-

drivers, any tool a team needs can be found in the roll-around, and there is usually more than one of each. Jacks, jack stands, alignment equipment, and scales are also in the garage area. The teams will have access to compressed air in the garage so they can take advantage of air tools.

With the setup complete, the first order of business is to get the car ready for practice and qualifying. Teams typically have a couple of hours of practice before qualifying, which usually takes place on Friday afternoon. The qualifying setup is one that is fast for one lap. As a result, the teams will do things during qualifying that they would never do during the race. A qualifying setup must only be fast for one or two laps, whereas a race setup must be fast for longer runs, the length being determined by

Practice time is limited, and all cars are not allowed on the track at the same time. The better use a team makes of its practice time, the better its chances to have a good run on race day.

the distance that the car can go on a full tank of fuel. Because of this, qualifying practice can be the most hectic practice of the weekend. The routine is to run a couple of laps, adjust the setup, then run a couple more laps and adjust again.

Since the cars are only on the track for a couple of laps, there is a great deal of traffic in the garage. This means more traffic in the transporter and more race cars for the team members to dodge as they whip in and out of the garage area. In recent years, as the competition has become tighter and more teams are attempting to qualify, a higher number of

teams do not make the race. The chance of not being fast enough to qualify for the race adds more pressure to this practice session.

Throughout qualifying practice, team members are constantly on the go, fetching springs, shocks, and other parts from the transporter. Crew chiefs spend their time running from the garage, where they can talk to their driver while the crew adjusts the race car, to the top of the hauler, where they can see the car run all of the way around the track. In most qualifying formats, the top 36 positions are determined on Friday based on speed. Places 37 to 43 are slotted with provisional

starters, based on owner's points.

When qualifying is complete, the teams begin preparation for race practice. A race setup is fast over many laps, not just one or two. During race practice, a team may make short runs at first, and once they feel that they have a good setup, the car is tested on longer runs.

The last practice before the race is "happy hour." This is a one-hour practice

Left: While the team is turning wrenches, the driver and crew chief discuss the car's performance and any changes that can improve it. The ability of a driver and crew chief to communicate is a critical component of success.

Below: Before qualifying, teams push their cars to the line. The qualifying order is determined by a blind draw.

Cars wait in line for their chance to qualify. Drivers are often out of breath after the run, not because of its length, but because of its intensity. The qualifying lap is run at the edge of the car's ability, and it will almost always be faster than the laps made under race conditions.

session that is typically held after the Saturday support race, and once again the garage becomes a busy place. Cars are adjusted, hit the track, and then are adjusted again. The result is a steady stream of race cars scooting in and out of the garage. Between runs, the teams make adjustments in the garage stall. Since practice time is limited, the quicker a team can make mechanical adjustments, the more practice runs its car can make on the track. When happy hour is over, cars don't hit the track again until the race.

If the team has a good setup during happy hour, it sleeps in peace the night before the race. If happy hour is problematic, the team may spend the night figuring out a new setup—and it will have to go into the race not knowing for certain how the car will perform.

When qualifying is complete, the cars are directed back off of the track, where a few items, such as the spoiler angle, are checked by officials before the car is allowed to go back to the garage.

CHAPTER FIVE

RACE DAY

W hen the sun rises on race day, the teams' efforts during the long hours of Friday and Saturday, and indeed the previous months, are soon to be put to the test on the track. However, there is still much to do on the morning of race day.

Pit Stall and Pit Cart

Early Sunday morning, teams begin to set up the pit stall, and a steady stream of team members winds from the garage to pit road, transporting equipment along the way. The outline of the pit-stall spaces is usually painted on the asphalt or concrete to mark the limits of each team's usable space. Early on race day, the teams arrange their gear around this perimeter, leaving as much room as possible for crew members to move around. Little space goes unused, as each team's gear fills its pit stall.

At a short track like Martinsville, the huge crowd's proximity to the on-track action adds an extra element of excitement to race day. *Nigel Kinrade*

The pit cart is the centerpiece of the pit stall and is the first piece of equipment to be set up. Pit carts are usually hand-built by the teams and are a blend of functionality and showmanship. The many items stored in the pit cart are those likely to be used during normal racing circumstances. Tools such as wrenches to adjust wedge or suspension parts are placed where they can be easily retrieved.

Modern pit carts will most likely house a television, VCR, and a satellite dish. If a team is running near the front, it can be helpful for a crew chief to watch his driver all the way around the track via television. Even if the team is not running up front, the broadcast may still be helpful, as crew chiefs are able to watch the leader's line around the track and see how it compares to his driver's. The VCR is used in conjunction with a video camera to record pit stops. The small camera is mounted on a boom and captures a view straight down over the pit stall. The pit cart also houses the air tanks, which supply the power for the air guns used to loosen and tighten lug nuts during pit stops.

Race morning begins with teams setting up the pit stall. Throughout the morning, there is a steady flow of equipment from the garage to the pits.

Above and opposite: A pit stall contains all of the essentials of racing. Tires, fuel, and tools are close at hand, ready for routine pit stops. Air tanks are contained in the pit cart and provide the power for the air guns.

The top of the pit cart is usually converted to a viewing platform for crew chiefs, owners, and occasionally a driver's wife. Due to the weight of the carts, they ride on large pneumatic tires so that they can traverse uneven ground with relative ease. A fold-up "T" bar is used to push or pull the cart and to turn the front wheels. Other essential gear includes lightweight aluminum jacks, jack stands, a water tank, hammers and pry bars (to fix body damage), bins with parts and tools, and countless tires. Most of the gear in the pit stall is essential to the operation of the car, but a few have creature comforts such as umbrellas and chairs. To top it all off, a few banners hang to ensure that if a team is running well and its pit stop is highlighted, the sponsors gets their money's worth.

Crash Cart

As race time draws near, teams, of course, hope for the best, but they must still prepare for the worst. The crash cart is a piece of equipment that the teams put a great deal of forethought into, yet they hope they won't have to use it. Stored on and in the crash cart are parts that are commonly damaged in "light" crashes, crashes that force the car off of the track but not out of the race. For instance, if the team suffers damage to the left front of the car, it is likely the oil cooler will be damaged, since it is mounted close behind the grille. This may

A lot of thought goes into creating a crash cart, though obviously teams hope that they will never use have to use it. The crash cart contains parts that can't be changed in the pits but are necessary if a wrecked car is not a complete write-off. While a crashed car may not win the race, it can still continue and accumulate points for the overall championship.

simply be a 10-minute repair, and if the team can change it during a yellow flag, it may not go too many laps down. As a result, an extra oil cooler and all of the mounting hardware are carried on the crash cart. Other items, such as suspension components, are also on the crash cart. Unlike the pit cart and the tool carts, the crash cart has no sides, doors, or drawers. As repairs will always be made under pressure situations, teams don't want to waste a second searching.

Tires are prepared for pit stops by gluing the lug nuts directly onto the rim, which facilitates routine changes on all four tires in less than 15 seconds.

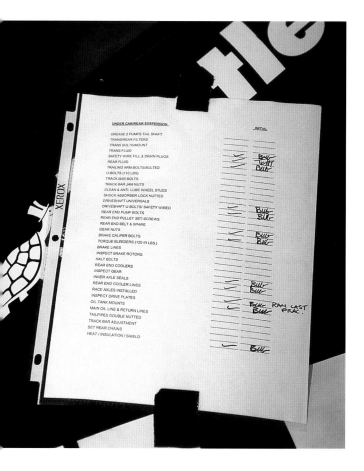

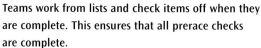

Teams work from lists and check items off when they are complete. This ensures that all prerace checks are complete.

The body of the car is receives a lot of attention during the inspection process. Height, width, length, and profile are all under tight control.

Checks and Balances

During the morning of the race, each team member will have specific items to check, whether they be related to the car, the pit stall, or media coordination. On the car, the crew chief, with the driver's input, decides the setup with which they will start the race. Crew members who are not busy setting up the pits will check and recheck the car. Lists with all of the tasks to be completed are taped to the car, and they are checked off when finished. Pit equipment such as air tools and jacks are also tested to make sure they are in perfect working order.

As the team works to get the car to the starting grid, the driver works on the "other side" of racing. On race-day morning, the drivers make multiple trips to sponsors' tents to chat with VIP fans, answer questions, and sign a few autographs. Later, the driver heads back to the motor coach or the transporter's lounge to get suited up. Each driver must also attend the drivers' meeting. If he doesn't, he will be moved to the back of the field to start the race.

As race time nears, each driver makes his way to the platform for driver introductions, which is followed by a lap around the track in a promotional car. Next, the drivers head back

Carburetors and air filters are also checked. Before and after the race, NASCAR battles the ingenious crews that occasionally find a way to go a bit faster without necessarily following the rule book.

to the pit road, finally able to put their full attention on the race and driving.

When the race starts, a driver's job is pretty simple: Go fast. In reality, though, driving fast is only part of the job. A driver must accurately communicate the car's handling so that adjustments can be made, especially if the car is handling poorly. Different drivers take different roles in this process. Some call in with the

Drivers are hard at work long before the green flag drops. They often spend the morning of race day meeting with sponsors and their guests. Only after they are suited up and are finished with the driver introductions are they finally able to concentrate on the race.

specific change, whether it is a round of wedge or a slight air-pressure adjustment. Others prefer to tell the crew chief what the car is doing and let the crew chief make the call. Either way, the ability of a driver and crew chief to communicate and adjust the race car is one of the greatest factors in determining whether that day is a success or a failure.

Race On!

Once the race begins, the team immediately evaluates how the car is handling and begins formulating an appropriate strategy. There are basically three states of handling: loose, tight, and just right. When a car is handling well, it basically means that it is neutral going through the turns—the front and rear of the car have equal levels of grip. If a car is loose, the back of the car wants to pass the front—the rear tires are losing grip and sliding laterally while the front tires are sticking and not sliding. Tight, on the other hand, means that the front tires are not gripping in the turn—when the driver tries to turn the car, it continues to slide forward. When the car is just right, or neutral, all four tires are sticking and the car glides smoothly through the turns. This is the Holy Grail of the crew chief.

Many things must come together to produce a winning setup for a race car. The geometry of the suspension, the spring rates, the shock combination, air pressures, and the downforce produced by the body all must be coordinated. A car that is good on long runs is usually a car with a winning setup.

A Winning Setup

A car must be right for a driver to put himself in a position to win. A winning setup starts in the shop with the construction of the car. The chassis and roll cage must be built with the highest degree of accuracy possible. All of the suspension

With so many days spent on the road, drivers have to find time to spend with their families whenever they can. As the sons of racers spend so much time around racing, it is no wonder that the sport continues to see subsequent generations of families on the track.

*Above:*Although Darlington was one of NASCAR's first superspeedway tracks, the egg-shaped oval is still considered very much a "handling" track, meaning the car's suspension setup is at least as important as its aerodynamic configuration. *Nigel Kinrade*

Below: At superspeedway races, like the Daytona 500, the cars run with reduced horsepower. This leads to tighter racing among packs of cars that run close together to better slice through the air. *Nigel Kinrade*

For road course events like the annual race at Sears Point, the teams must set up their cars to turn both right and left.
Nigel Kinrade

mounting points are determined during the construction process.

Next is the body. When the body is put on, it must be built with maximum aerodynamic efficiency. For years, teams worried most about their cars' aerodynamics at Daytona and Talladega, but the truth is that during any race at any track, the only period of time that aerodynamics are not important is when the car is sitting still during a pit stop. But the ability to fine-tune a car during the race is an important factor in victory. How many times have you seen drivers like Jeff Gordon, Jeff Burton, and Tony Stewart run poorly at the beginning of a race but improve as the day goes on?

Handling
Handling is everything in Winston Cup racing. Some engines generate a bit more power than others, and that helps, but day in and day

out, it is the best-handling car that wins the race. A good demonstration of this was the 1999 New Hampshire race. In response to the fatal crashes of Adam Petty and Kenny Irwin, NASCAR officials mandated that the race be run with the dreaded restrictor plate, a device previously only used at Daytona and Talladega. The results were interesting. While some reported that the plate dropped horsepower in the cars from about 750 to 450, the qualifying speed only dropped a few miles per hour.

Tires

All the roads of handling lead to the tires. Handling is ultimately determined by what happens in the small contact patch between the tire and the pavement. Everything changed when the radial came to stock-car racing. Before Goodyear introduced the racing radial tire, racing tires were bias ply tires. In bias ply tires, the cords, which give a tire its strength, were run at an angle from bead to bead. On a radial tire, the cords run straight across the tread from bead to bead. This difference in construction has a huge impact on how the tire behaves during a race. Bias ply tires were not nearly as stable as the radial tire. When a bias ply tire was put on the car, its characteristics changed during a run. As the tire wore and the heat increased, the tire tended to grow (the diameter of the tire increased). What this meant was that regardless of how the car was set up, it constantly changed. As each tire was experiencing different conditions (the right-front takes much more abuse than the left-rear), they grew at different rates. So, during a 50-lap run, the stagger and air pressure were constantly changing; thus the way the car handled was constantly changing. As a result, driver skill was a paramount. Throughout a run, the driver was forced to search for different lines around the racetrack to get the car to work well. When the sport began to use radials, this situation changed.

As a radial builds up heat, the air pressure in the tire changes and the tire stiffens up, just like putting more spring in the car. Other than that, though, the tire stays relatively stable; thus a setup does not change as dramatically during long runs. This being the case, a car's design assembly and suspension tuning became more and more critical to the overall performance. Today, it is how the suspension takes care of the tire that the team focuses on in a setup.

After pit stops, the temperatures of the removed tires are taken. By comparing these temperatures, the crew chief can determine how the tires are wearing. As much as possible, the temperatures should be within a close range on all four corners. If one is too high, the car may be fast for a few laps but slow dramatically when the tire gets too hot, or a too-hot tire may even blow and cause the car to hit the wall.

When a new set of tires starts a run, the friction between the racing surface and the tire heats the rubber, making it softer. It is this soft rubber, as well as the heavy sidewall construction, that allow cars to achieve such high speeds in the turns. It is this grip that usually decides the winner of a race.

Tire wear differs depending on the type of track being raced. Tracks like Darlington are hard on tires, whereas Talladega is not. For safety reasons, tires incorporate an inner liner—a small, heavy-duty inner tube mounted on the rim inside the racing tire. In the case of a blowout, this inner liner should retain its air pressure and keep the rim from digging into the pavement and causing the car to flip.

A well-handling race car is one that best counters the physics being exerted on it at the track. This ultimately boils down to how the stress is distributed around the four tires. The better the distribution, the better the tire wear.

For all racers, weight is the enemy. The elimination of weight is a good thing, up until the point where a part would fail. Teams cannot, however, totally realize their weight-saving efforts. All cars must meet the minimum weight specification before entering the track. If the car weighs less than the specification, the team must add ballast in order to pass the weigh-in. However, by lightening up areas of the car, teams are able to decide where the extra weight is placed. For handling purposes, putting the ballast between the wheel wells (preferably on the left side of the car) is better than placing it closer to an end of the car. Provisions have also been made to factor in the driver's weight. Drivers weighing less than 200 pounds must add weight to the car in 10-pound increments, up to a maximum of 50 pounds. For instance, a 175-pound driver will add 30 pounds. This weight may be added to the left side of the car. After the race, the car must be within .5 percent of the minimum weight of the car at the start of the race.

Aerodynamics

Other than weight, one of the biggest factors that impacts handling and speed is the aerodynamic efficiency of a race car's body. The more aerodynamic the body is, the less resistance the car encounters and the faster the car can go.

The aerodynamics of the car body have become so refined that a single piece of tape can change the handling. If a piece of tape is removed from the grille, more air enters the grille, which increases the lift on the front end and takes pressure, or downforce, off of the front of the car.

There are two primary aerodynamic forces that the teams work with on the race car: drag and downforce. Drag is simply the resistance that the air puts on the car as it moves. Just as a boat displaces water as the hull moves through the water, a race car displaces air. The more efficiently the body cuts through the air, the higher the speed that can be attained with a given amount of horsepower.

A simple example of this can be seen by sticking your hand out the window while driving at highway speeds. If you position your hand flat against the wind, palm forward, the resistance can easily be felt as your hand is forced back by the air. But if you rotate your hand 90 degrees so that your forefinger forms the leading edge, there is much less resistance, or drag, as the same shape moves through the air. The sleeker the body the better.

Downforce, on the other hand, is the amount of downward pressure the air puts on the car as it passes over the car. On the front of the car, the nose, hood, and tops of the fenders facilitate this, while on the rear, the spoiler enhances this. Again, use the hand-out-the-window example. If you keep it flat, there is little or no force pushing your hand up or down. Rotate it a bit, though, turning the front of your hand down, and the wind will force your hand down. The more you tilt, the stronger the downforce. Downforce is a great friend when it comes to handling. As the air pushes down on the body and spoiler, the car will handle better. However, there is a cost. The better the downforce, the worse the drag. Likewise, the lower the drag, the lower the downforce. Thus, a compromise must be made and some balance achieved.

On a track like Talladega, teams give up some downforce, as handling is not as much of an issue, and work to eliminate drag. However, at a track like Indianapolis, where the turns are long and flat, the teams will try for downforce and deal with the extra drag. Teams must balance the front and rear downforce so that the car turns evenly or neutrally through the turn. Too much front downforce and not enough

On the rear, the spoiler provides the downforce. Thus, like the profile of the front of the car, it is closely monitored by NASCAR.

rear will make the car loose, whereas too much rear and not enough front will make it push.

The reliance on downforce to make a car handle well has resulted in a new term on the circuit: aero push. Often, especially on flat tracks with one groove, a car may run well in the lead with no cars in front of it. This is known as having clean air. But if the car gets behind another car, it isn't as fast and may not be capable of passing. The cause of this is the dreaded aero push. When a car is in clean air, the downforce on the front of the car is at its maximum and is balanced with the rear downforce, which allows the car to turn neutrally, without being loose or tight. When behind another car, however, the downforce on the car is weakened due to the air action coming off of the rear of the car in front. As a result, the downforce on the rear of the car is greater than the downforce on the front, and the front tires lose grip. This makes the car not want to turn and push out to the wall.

With four different makes currently racing on the Winston Cup circuit, NASCAR officials are constantly working to keep parity between the bodies of all four makes. It is a difficult proposition. In general, they use spoiler size and the front bumper's kickout to balance the makes. If the officials see that one make is at a disadvantage (through race results and wind-tunnel testing), they will grant a concession. This is both good news and bad news for a team. The good news is that they get some relief. The bad news is they have to cut up the race cars, rebuild them to the new specifications, and then figure out how the changes will affect the balance of the race car. If they get a bit more kickout, which adds downforce to the car, they will have to see how this increase will change the known handling characteristics of the car.

Pit-Stop Adjustments

When a car starts a run after a pit stop, and the tires are new and sticky, a setup that is off a bit may run very well. This is often seen during a race when a car will be very fast for 20 or so laps and then begin to fade when the car cannot overcome a flaw in its setup. Races can be won with a setup like this, but the cautions must fall at the right time. The guys who have really nailed the setup will be the ones who run the more consistent laps throughout the run. Winston Cup cars have become so refined that the adjustments made during pit stops are relatively minor.

To optimize the tire–pavement connection, the crew chief has a number of areas on the car that he can adjust. The first is the spring rate. Springs are categorized by spring rate, which is a measure of the resistance a spring exerts when compressed, and it is measured in pounds of force per inch of compression. Because of the importance of springs in making a car handle well, crews test many combinations of spring rates on various corners of the car. On all tracks except road courses, a setup will have a different spring rate at each corner of the car to counter the particular forces that a track applies to the car as it turns. For instance, at Dover, the force on the right front tire is about 3,500 pounds, essentially equal to the entire weight of the car, which forces the team to run a very stiff spring on the right front. At a short, flat track, there is much less weight on the right front, and the teams will run a much softer spring. The springs on all four corners are determined during practice and are not changed during the race. However, the crew chief can still change the way the springs work by making a wedge adjustment. As described in chapter 3, the coil springs on both the front and rear of the car are held in place on the top with adjustable fittings. As the bolt in the fitting is turned, it either tightens or loosens, which either compresses or decompresses the spring. The compression and extension of the springs change the way the car's weight is distributed to each corner. Thus, this adjustment can change the way the car handles. Since the wedge adjustment points on the front of the car cannot be accessed without lifting the hood, the adjustments made during pit stops are to the rear. The bolts are accessed through a small tube that runs from the rear window to the jack

Left: Teams experiment with different spring rates during practice but must decide on a set before the race. The time needed to change even a single spring would put a car many laps down if done during the race.

Below: Like the springs, shock selection is a critical choice. Shocks can be rebuilt, adjusted, and tested at a custom workstation in the transporter.

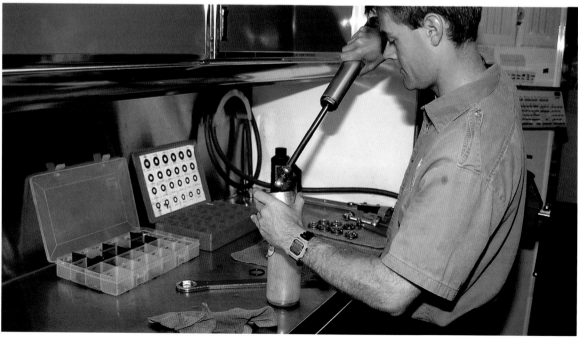

bolt. A wedge adjustment takes no more than a second or two during a pit stop and does not delay the driver.

Teams may also insert or take out a spring rubber. These rubber pieces fit between the coils of the spring and stiffen it up. Teams will often start the race with a spring rubber and pull it out if they need to decrease the spring rate. Another way to fine-tune the spring rate is with an air pressure adjustment. As a rule, an increase of 1 pound of air pressure will result in an increase of about 10 pounds of spring pressure. Likewise, dropping the tire pressure lowers the spring rate. At times, teams may make changes as small as 1/4 pound of air pressure. This fine line concerning air pressure is why teams designate tire specialists to keep track of tire wear and tire pressures. A trip to pit road always means a tire specialist checking and rechecking the tire pressures before the tires go on the car. A mistake in air pressure can hurt the handling of the car as much as a purposeful adjustment can help it.

At one time, competitors could run two shocks per wheel, but with the recent advances in shock absorber technology, this is no longer allowed. Modern shock absorbers are able to handle the load with just one shock per wheel. In the last 10 years, finding the perfect shock combination has become an obsession with Winston Cup crew chiefs. Many times, Tony Stewart has given a lion's share of credit for the team's success to his shock builder. Shock absorbers are tuned just like most other parts of the car. A shock dyno is used to test the shock's performance, which is centered on compression and rebound. This refers to how much force is required to push the shock in (compression) and the force the shock exerts pushing back out (rebound). This means that the shocks are integral components that are responsible for keeping the all-important tire contact patch in touch with the track. If a tire is hopping and skipping, it can't grip. Teams can fine-tune the shock to achieve the compression and rebound combination they desire. This area is closely monitored and shocks are liable to be disassembled and inspected by NASCAR officials.

On all cars, the rear shocks must be located inside the frame. For many years, the teams have had to have many shock combinations for each track, and a shock dyno can be found in each hauler. This device allows the teams to see exactly how the shock is performing before they mount it on the car.

Another handling adjustment is stagger. While the radial tires are much more stable and uniform than the old bias ply tires, they can still be a bit different in size. Stagger refers to the difference in circumference of the right-side tire and the left-side tire. If all of the tires are the same size, the car will roll straight forward, just like a rolling pin. However, if the tires on one side are bigger than on the other side, the car rolls more like a lightbulb, which may help it turn through the corner better.

Fifteen Seconds

While the driver's action on the track goes a long way in determining the team's finishing position, pit work can greatly aid or hinder a driver. A good pit stop starts as the car comes down from racing speed. The first section of the pit stop begins when the driver begins to decrease from race speed, and it ends when he reaches the point where the pit road speed limit begins. The shorter the time to accomplish this the better. Occasionally, a car will lock the brakes and spin when coming into the pits, a result of trying a bit too hard to accomplish this task.

The second stage of the pit stop is from the beginning of pit road until the car stops in the pits. As the pit road speed is limited by

The choreography of a pit stop, where teams now routinely change four tires and add 22 gallons of fuel in 13 to 15 seconds, though it has been accomplished in less than 13 seconds. Here, the Ganassi/Sabates team executes a quick two-tire stop.

NASCAR, the driver must go as close as he can to the speed limit without going over, which will result in a penalty.

The third phase is the pit stop itself, the total time it takes for seven guys to change four tires and add 22 gallons of fuel.

The fourth and final phase is the driver's acceleration from a stop to the time he reaches race speed. The importance of the first, second, and fourth stages of a pit stop is often overlooked by casual observers.

When the car stops in the pit box, the action begins. On a four-tire stop, the jack man will go to the passenger side and, with one

stroke of the custom aluminum jack, he will lift the right side off of the ground. Each tire changer removes the lug nuts, pulls the tire off, gets the new tire from the tire carrier (who locates it on the studs), and tightens it. Meanwhile, the tire carrier keeps the old tire from rolling away, which is a penalty offense. Once the tires are on the right side, the jack man releases the jack, dropping the car. He then runs around the front of the car and jacks up the left side, and the process repeats itself.

While this is going on, the gas man is emptying two 11-gallon cans of fuel into the car while the catch-can man contains any fuel overflow. When all of this is complete, the jack man drops the left side of the car, which is the driver's signal to take off. It is considered successful if all of this is done in 13 to 15 seconds.

That's all it takes! Millions of dollars up front to start the team; success to sell sponsorship; sponsorship to fund success, assemble talent, keep talent; and stay away from bad

luck. The guys you see standing in Victory Lane each Sunday afternoon are the ones who did it for that seven-day stretch. Those who sit in the place of honor at the annual Winston Cup Championship dinner are the ones who did it all year.

This is what it's all about: A trip to victory lane. Here Jimmie Johnson celebrates his 2002 win at California Speedway. *Nigel Kinrade*

INDEX

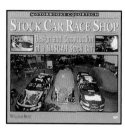

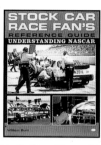

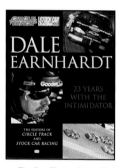

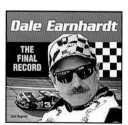